Children's Books and Reading

Montrose Jonas Moses

Alpha Editions

This edition published in 2024

ISBN : 9789367246252

Design and Setting By
Alpha Editions
www.alphaedis.com
Email - info@alphaedis.com

As per information held with us this book is in Public Domain.
This book is a reproduction of an important historical work. Alpha Editions uses the best technology to reproduce historical work in the same manner it was first published to preserve its original nature. Any marks or number seen are left intentionally to preserve its true form.

Contents

INTRODUCTORY NOTE ....- 1 -
I. THE PROBLEM..- 2 -
THE GROWTH OF JUVENILE LITERATURE..................- 11 -
II. THE RISE OF CHILDREN'S BOOKS ....- 13 -
III. THE OLD-FASHIONED LIBRARY ....- 37 -
IV. CONCERNING NOW AND THEN ....- 80 -
V. THE LIBRARY AND THE BOOK.................................- 95 -
VI. APPENDIX..- 113 -

INTRODUCTORY NOTE

In the course of preparing the material for the following sketch, I was brought into very agreeable relations with many persons whose practical experience in library work proved of exceptional value to me. I wish to take this means of thanking Miss Annie Carroll Moore, Supervisor of Children's Rooms in the New York Public Library, and Mr. C. G. Leland, Supervisor of School Libraries and member of the New York Board of Education, for every encouragement and assistance.

To Miss Caroline M. Hewins of the Hartford Public Library, Miss Frances Jenkins Olcott of the Pittsburgh Carnegie Library, Miss Caroline Burnite of the Cleveland Public Library, the Reverend Joseph McMahon, a member of the Advisory Board of the New York Public Library, Mr. Frederic W. Erb of the Columbia University Library, and to Mr. Tudor Jenks, I am indebted for general advice.

In special lines, I had the privilege of consultation with Mr. Frank Damrosch, Mr. C. Whitney Coombs, and Miss Kate Cohen for music; Miss Emilie Michel for French; and Miss Hedwig Hotopf for German.

The librarians of Columbia University, the Pratt Institute, and the Astor Library have rendered me marked service for which I am grateful.

I wish to thank the New York *Outlook*, *Independent*, and *Evening Post* for affording me opportunities to publish from time to time data relating to juvenile books and reading.

Finally, I wish to fix the responsibility for whatever statements are made in the way of criticism upon myself; this is only due to those whose extensive knowledge of the subject is being exerted in a professional capacity; and to those many authors whose books and papers are indicated in the bibliographical notes.

M. J. M.

NEW YORK, August, 1907.

I.
THE PROBLEM

Any good book, any book that is wiser than yourself, will teach you some things.—Carlyle, to an unknown correspondent, March 13, 1843.

Therfore I pray that no man Reprehende

This lytyl Book, the whiche for you I make;

But where defaute ys, latte ylke man amende,

And nouhte deme yt; [I] pray thaym for youre sake.

—*The Babees Book.*

The field of children's books is by no means an uninterrupted host of dancing daffodils; it is not yellow with imperishable gold. In fact, there is a deplorable preponderance of the sere and yellow leaf. Yet there is no fairer opportunity for the writer than that which offers itself in the voluntary spirit of a boy or girl reader. Here are to be met no crotchets or fads, no prejudices or unthinkable canons of art. Because the body is surcharged with surplus energy necessary to growth, because the mind is throwing out delicate tendrils that foreshadow its potential future, one realises how vital is the problem of children's reading, how significant the manner in which it is being handled.

At the outset, it is essential for us to distinguish between theory, history, and practice. The field, with all its rich soil, is in need of weeding. Not so very long ago, it lay unrecognised by the library, as of sufficient importance for separate and specialised consideration. But now, with the prominence being given to children's reading-rooms, the field needs to be furrowed. Let us not ignore the salubrious under-stratum of the past; it has served its mission in asserting the claims of childhood; it has both negatively and positively marked the individuality of childhood, in a distinctive juvenile literature. Perhaps the writers who were inspired by the Rousseau doctrine of education, and those who abetted the Sunday-school movement of the last century, were deceived in their attitude; for they considered the machinery by which they hoped to mould character, rather than the nature of the heart and soul upon which they were actually working. A right action, a large, human, melodramatic deed, are more healthy for boys and girls than all the reasons that could be given for them. In literature for children, as in life, the moral *habit* should be unquestioning. All leading educators and ethical teachers recognise this fact.

The whole matter simply resolves itself into a difference in viewpoint between the past and present. Smile as we must over the self-conscious piousness of early juvenile literature, it contained a great deal of sincerity; it did its pioneer work excellently well. To the writer of children's books, to the home, where one essential duty is personal guidance, to the librarian whose work is not the science of numbers, but a profession of culture-distributing, some knowledge of the past harvests from this field would appear indispensable. For the forgotten tales of long ago, the old-fashioned stories represent something more than stained pages and crude woodcuts, than stilted manners and seeming priggishness; they stand for the personal effort and service of men and women striving with staunch purpose in the interests of childhood, however mistaken their estimates of this childhood may have been. These books, to the library, are so much fallow material as a practical circulating proposition, but they represent forces significant in the history of children's books. I would much rather see a librarian fully equipped with a knowledge of Miss Edgeworth's life, of her human associations, together with the inclinations prompting her to write "The Parent's Assistant," than have her read a whole list of moral tales of the same purport and tone.

The immediate problem, therefore, necessitates a glance at this field of children's literature, and some knowledge of its essential details. It involves a contact with books of all grades; it calls into play, with the increasing number of libraries, and with the yearly addition of children's rooms, a keen discerning judgment on the part of the librarian, not only as to child nature, but as to the best methods of elimination, by which bad books may be separated from good, and by which the best may preponderate. But the librarian is not the only factor; the parent and the writer also come into account. They, too, must share a responsibility which will be more fully determined later on, but which now means that they both owe the child an indispensable duty; the one in giving to the growing boy or girl most intelligent guidance along the path of fullest development; the other in satisfying this need—not in deflecting juvenile taste by means of endless mediocrity and mild sentimentalism. It is an unfortunate circumstance that the effects of mediocrity are longer-lived than the immediate evil itself.

In the problem of children's reading we must consider two aspects; there is the bogey image of a theoretical or sociological or educational child, and also the book as a circulating commodity. There is the machinery of "The Child"; Dr. Isaac Watts shaped one; Jean Jacques Rousseau another; the Edgeworths still another, and now the psychologist's framework of childhood, more subtle, more scientific, more interesting, threatens us everywhere. But no patent has so far supplanted the fundamental excellence of human nature. There are assuredly demarkations and successive steps in elementary education, but are not these becoming too specialised? Since we are dealing with the Boy and the Story rather than with the Scholar and the Text-book, with culture which is personal, and not with expediency, we needs must choose the human model in preference to all others.

And so it is with the choice of the librarian. In dealing with books in the bulk, there is a tendency to emphasise system above the humanising excellence of what the books contain. After all the mechanical detail is done, when the cover has been labelled, when the catalogue notation has been figured, when the class distribution has been determined, the librarian stands middleman in a threefold capacity. She is a purveyor, in the sense that she passes a book over the counter; she is a custodian, in so far as books need protection; she is the high priestess, since the library is a temple of treasures, a storehouse for our literary heritage. In any library, whether it be yours at home, with your own books upon the shelves, or the public's, with volumes representing so much of your taxation on which you base your citizenship, the rare companionship of books is one of their humanising qualities. This is as much a truth for children as for grown-ups.

With the fear that there is an effort on the part of many to crystallise reading into a science, comes the necessity to foster a love of reading for its own sake. The democracy of books has grown larger with the cheapening process of manufacture; while the establishment of public libraries offers to every one an equal privilege. In an assemblage of many books, a certain spiritual dignity should attach itself to the utilitarian fact.

There is no definition for children's books; the essential point is appeal, interest. As far back as 1844, a writer in the *Quarterly Review* very aptly claimed that "a genuine child's book is as little like a book for grown people cut down, as the child himself is like a little old man." Peculiarly, there is a popular misconception that an author of juveniles advances in art only when he or she leaves off penning stories or fairy tales, and begins publishing novels. On the face of it, this is absurd. Like any other gift, writing for children cannot be taught; it has to be born. If possible, with the exception of drama, it is the most difficult art to master, since its narrative will not stand imitation, since its simplicity must represent naturalness and not effort, since its meaning must be within reach, and without the tone of condescension.

Professor Richard Burton has written: "A piece of literature is an organism, and should, therefore, be put before the scholar, no matter how young, with its head on, and standing on both feet." This injunction applies to all books. Where the classics excel is in their very fulness and honesty of narrative. Can the same be said of our "series" brand?

The writing of children's books is more aptly phrased the writing of books for children. There was a time when such books, as a class by themselves, were unknown; yet boys and girls expanded, and perhaps remembered more of what they read than they do to-day, although they were not taught as much. There are some pessimists, not so unwise in their pessimism, who believe that if less emphasis was bestowed upon the word *children*, and more upon the word *literature*, the situation would be materially bettered.

Can we recall any of our great men—literary, scientific, or otherwise—who were brought up on distinctively juvenile literature. A present-day boy who would read what Lamb or Wordsworth, Coleridge or Tennyson, Gladstone or Huxley devoured with gusto in their youth, would set the psychologists in a flutter, would become an object for head-lines in our papers. There is a mistaken conception regarding what are children's books, in the best sense of the word. A standard which might have excellent conservative results, although it would be thoroughly one-sided and liable to false interpretation, could be based on the assertion that those books only are children's classics which can be relished by a grown-up public. "Alice in Wonderland," "The Water Babies," "Peter Pan"—such stories have a universal appeal. And it is well to remember that at least five of the world's classics, not originally written for children, have been appropriated by them: "The Arabian Nights"; "Pilgrim's Progress"; "Robinson Crusoe"; "Gulliver's Travels"; "Baron Münchausen."

With the reading democracy created by public libraries, there has developed the need for this special kind of writing. Excesses have unfortunately arisen such as made a critic once exclaim in disgust, "Froissart is cut into spoon-meat, and Josephus put into swaddling clothes." While we shall, in the following pages, find many odd theories and statements regarding simplification of style, it is as well to be forearmed against this species of writing. Democracy in literature is falsely associated with mediocrity. When one reads the vitiating "series" class of story-book, the colourless college record, the diluted historical narrative, there is cause for despair. But there is no need for such cheapening. The wrong impression is being created in the popular mind that literature is synonymous with dulness; that only current fiction is worth while. And we find children confessing that they rarely read non-fiction, a term they only dimly comprehend. It is not right that a middle-class population should have relegated to it a middle-class literature. Such, however, at the present moment, seems to be the situation. And as a consequence all departments suffer. Except for a very few volumes, there is no biography for children that is worthy of endorsement, for the simple reason that the dignity of a whole life, its meaning and growth, are subordinated to the accentuation of a single incident. History becomes a handmaiden to the slender story. Let those writers who are looking for an unworked vein ponder this. The fictionising of all things is one of the causes for this poverty; the text-book habit another.

The poet Blake sings:

"Thou hast a lap full of seed,

And this is a fine country.

Why dost thou not cast thy seed,

And live in it merrily?"

But, though we are repeatedly casting our seed in the field of juvenile literature, we are not reaping the full harvest, because we are not living in the land of childhood merrily.

Start as you will to treat of children's books as the mere vehicle for giving joy, and education will pursue you. Acknowledging all the benefits that the moral tale and the instructive walk have bestowed, we know not which to pity most—the child in a moral strait-jacket, or the child observing nature! The terms we use in describing these writers of a past generation are always the same; they are not prepossessing, though they may sound quaint. We turn from such critical phrases as "flabby treatment of the Bible," "dear, didactic, deadly dull" Mrs. Barbauld, Miss Edgeworth's "overplus of sublime purpose," to definite terms of protest such as those of the "Professor at the Breakfast Table," condemning the little meek sufferers with their spiritual exercises, and those of Emerson ending in his cry of "What right have you to *one* virtue!" The mistaken attitude, which has slipped from the moral to the educational sphere, seems to be that self-development is not just as important as prescribed courses. While the latter are necessary to the school, the librarian must reckon differently; for, to her, the child is not so much a class as a unit.

Elementary education is marked by the compulsory factor; in reading, a child's interest is voluntary. On the other hand, the severity of a Puritan Sunday, the grimness of a New England Primer, developed in childhood sound principles of righteousness; they erected a high fence between heaven and hell. But the moral tale utilised "little meannesses of conventional life," suggested sly deceit and trivial pettiness; it quibbled and its ethics were often doubtful. The reaction that followed let slip a valuable adjunct in culture; to-day the knowledge of the Bible in schools and colleges is appallingly shallow; this fact was revealed in the results of an examination or test held by President Thwing some years ago. Dr. Felix Adler, pleading from the non-sectarian platform, asks for the re-establishment of ethics in our schools as a study of social relations, and for the extended use of Bible stories, shorn of religious meaning, yet robbed of none of their essential strength or beauty or truth. The librarian has wisely mapped out for her story hour such a course, gleaned from the parables, and from the vast treasure houses of narrative abounding in both Testaments and in fables.

Turn to your colleges and your schools, and you will find that, generally speaking, there is dug a deep channel between literature and life, which has no right to be. We should study our ethics as one of the inherent elements in poetry and in prose. The moral *habit* is part of the structure of the Arthurian legends.

Since the time of Rousseau the emancipation of the child has steadily advanced; in society, he has taken his place. No longer is it incumbent upon him to be seen and not heard, no longer are his answers written out for him to memorise. Mr. E. V. Lucas, in the preface to his "Forgotten Tales of Long Ago," calls attention to one story, "Ellen and George; or, The Game at Cricket," culled from "Tales for Ellen," by Alicia Catherine Mant, and in a characteristically droll manner he says, "Ellen's very sensible question (as it really was) on p. 184, 'Then why don't you send the cat away?' is one of the first examples of independent—almost revolutionary—thought in a child, recorded by a writer for children in the early days."

But the chains that have fallen from one door have been threatening to shackle another. Where once children could scarcely escape the moral, their imaginations now have no room for flight. Fancy is bestrided by fact. We must give reasons for everything. When Artemus Ward was asked why the summer flowers fade, he exclaimed, "Because it's their biz, let 'em fade." In nature study for children the general effect leaves a deeper impression than the technical structure. We do not know whether it is necessary to have Mr. Seton's "Story of Wahb" vouched for as to accuracy in every detail. The scientific naturalists and story-writers are constantly wrangling, but there is not so much harm done to nature after all. An author who wilfully perverts fact, who states as true for the class what he knows to be a variant in the one coming under his observation, should be called to account. Otherwise a human interest attached to animals creates a wide appeal. But to use this vehicle for exploiting the commonplace, and what properly belongs to the text-book, should be condemned by the librarian. Mr. Tudor Jenks[1] humorously declares: "We ask our little ones to weep over the tribulations of a destitute cock-roach or a bankrupt tumble-bug." And another critic of an earlier age writes of those same children—"They are delighted, it is true, with the romantic story of 'Peter, the wild boy,' but they have not the slightest curiosity to know the natural history, or Linnæan nomenclature of the pig-nuts he ate."

The following pages have been written after some extensive investigation. Within the past few years, about fifteen hundred of the latest books for children have come to my desk; they have not been without meaning for the present, or without connection with the past. While it has not been the intention to write a full history of children's books, some idea is given of the extent and possibilities of the field; the historical development is sketched in outline. There is need for a comprehensive volume. In addition, an attempt is here made to reconcile system with culture; to discover what the library is aiming to do with juvenile readers in the community; to show the relation which the Library, the School, and the Home, bear, one to the other, and all to the child. Having carefully examined lists of books recommended by libraries for children of all ages and grades, a limited number of volumes, marked by an excellence which makes them worthy of preservation, is recommended as suitable for boys and girls. These titles are given in an appendix. The fault with most lists of this character is that they too often represent the choice of one person. To counteract this one-sidedness, the co-operation of an advisory board was obtained, marked by wide experience, by an intimate contact with and knowledge of the books considered, and by a desire to show a human respect for the tastes of children.

There are certain phases in the consideration of the departments that have been suggested by young readers themselves. The desire for books about musicians, and for piano and violin scores, brought to light the lack of any guaranteed assemblage of songs which, in variety, in quality, in sentiment and imagination, might be called distinctive. The interest in a certain type of drawing as shown by the juvenile demand for Boutet de Monvel, Kate Greenaway, and Caldecott picture-books, suggested the advisability of including a full list of these publications.[2] One cannot approach the subject with any ironclad rules, yet it is always profitable to heed experiments based on common sense. The results of such experiments are but mileposts in the general advance; they must not be taken as final. Yet it is well to experiment in order to avoid crystallisation.

Children are entitled to their full heritage; education is paramount, culture is the saving grace. Your memory of a child is the healthy glow of the unfettered spirit. None of us want him with a book in his hand all the time. We wish him to take the freshness of life as his nature, to run with hair tossing to the wind. But glance into his eyes and you will find a craving look that a ball will not satisfy, a far-away expression that no shout from the roadside will change. It is the placid gleam of sunset after physical storm, the moment of rest after the overflow of animal energy. Children have their hero moments when they are not of the present, but are part of that perennial truth which is clearer-visioned in the past, since we have to dream of it. Kate Douglas Wiggin claims that the book is a fact to a child. It should be an idealising fact.

Not long ago a crazy man died, after having drawn up a will: his world's goods consisted of the wide, wide world; his legatees were every living soul. He said:

"I leave to children, inclusively, but only for the term of their childhood, all and every, the flowers of the fields, and the blossoms of the woods, with the right to play among them freely, according to the customs of children, warning them at the same time against thistles and thorns. And I devise to children the banks of the brooks, and the golden sands beneath the waters thereof, and the odors of the willows that dip therein, and the white clouds that float high over the giant trees. And I leave the children the long, long days to be merry in, in a thousand ways, and the night and the moon and the train of the milky way to wonder at."

What thinks the teacher of such riches, what the librarian with her catalogue number? A book is a fact, nay, a friend, a dream. Is there not a creed for us all in the wisdom of that crazy man? Here was one with clear vision, to whom fact was as nothing before the essential of one's nature—a prophet, a seer, one to whom the tragedy of growing up had been no tragedy, but whose memory of childhood had produced a chastening effect upon his manhood. Are we surprised to find him adding:

"I give to good fathers and mothers, in trust for their children, all good little words of praise and encouragement, and all quaint pet names and endearments, and I charge said parents to use them justly and generously, as the needs of their children may require."

And so, we ask, more especially the parent than the librarian, is there not excitement in the very drawing out from a child his heart's desire? Imperative it is in all cases that book-buying should not be a lottery, but more persistently apparent does it become that a child's *one* individual book upon the Christmas-tree or for a birthday should not represent a grown-up's afterthought.

Bibliographical Note

The articles referred to in this chapter are:

BURTON, RICHARD Literature for Children. *No. Amer.* 167:278 (Sept., 1898).

CHILDREN'S BOOKS—[From the *Quarterly Review.*] *Liv. Age*, 2:1–12 (Aug. 10, 1841).

THWING, CHARLES F.—Significant Ignorance About the Bible as Shown Among College Students of Both Sexes. *Century*, 60:123–128 (May, 1900).

FOOTNOTES

[1] Mr. Jenks, besides editing for *St. Nicholas Magazine* during many years a unique department known as "Books and Reading," has written widely on the subject of juvenile literature. See his "The Modern Child as a Reader." *The Book-buyer*, August, 1901, p. 17.

[2] An interesting field for research is that of the illustration of children's books. Note Thomas Bewick, John Bewick, etc. Of a later period, Tenniel, Cruikshank, Doré, Herr Richter. *Vide* "The Child and His Book," Mrs. E. M. Field, chap. xiv; "Some Illustrators of Children's Books." Also "Children's Books and their Illustrators." Gleeson White, *The International Studio*. Special Winter No., 1897–98.

THE GROWTH OF JUVENILE LITERATURE

A PARTIAL INDICATION, BY DIAGRAM

FRENCH IMPETUS

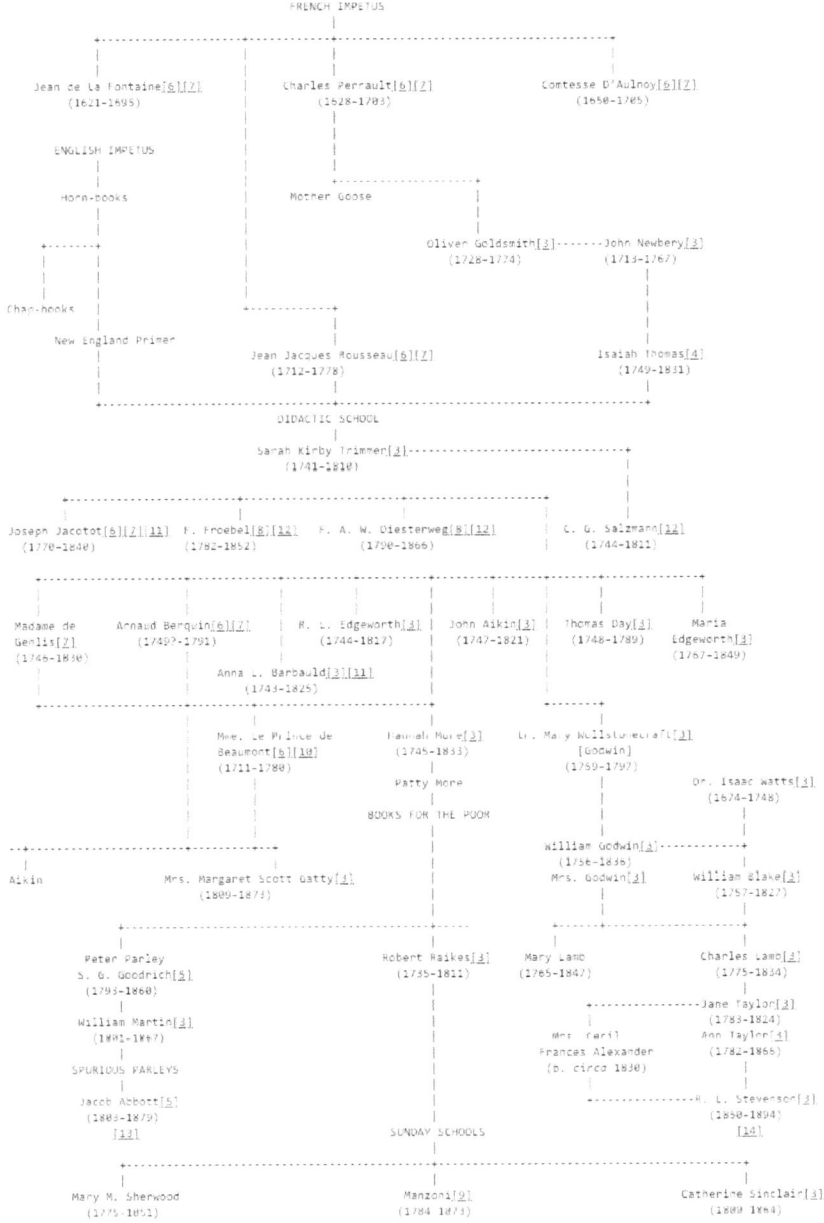

FOOTNOTES

[3] Dictionary of National Biography. Gives further bibliography.

[4] Appleton's Biographical Dictionary.

[5] Lamb's Biographical Dictionary.

[6] Nouvelle Biographie Générale. Gives further bibl.

[7] La Grande Encyclopédie. Gives further bibl.

[8] Meyers Konversations-Lexikon. Bibl.

[9] Diccionario Enciclopedico Hispano-Americano.

[10] Influence of Perrault.

[11] Sister of John Aikin.

[12] Influence of Rousseau.

[13] American End of the Development.

[14] English End of the Development.

II.
THE RISE OF CHILDREN'S BOOKS

I wish Mrs. Marcet, the Right Honourable T. B. Macaulay, or any other person possessing universal knowledge, would take a toy and child's emporium in hand, and explain to us all the geographical and historical wonders it contains. That Noah's ark, with its varied contents—its leopards and lions, with glued pump-handled tails; its light-blue elephants and ⊥ footed ducks—that ark containing the cylindrical family of the patriarch—was fashioned in Holland, most likely, by some kind pipe-smoking friends of youth by the side of a slimy canal. A peasant in a Danubian pine-wood carved that extraordinary nutcracker, who was painted up at Nuremberg afterwards in the costume of a hideous hussar. That little fir lion, more like his roaring original than the lion at Barnet, or the lion of Northumberland House, was cut by a Swiss shepherd boy tending his goats on a mountainside, where the chamois were jumping about in their untanned leather. I have seen a little Mahometan on the Etmeidan at Constantinople twiddling about just such a whirligig as you may behold any day in the hands of a small Parisian in the Tuileries Gardens. And as with the toys, so with the toy books. They exist everywhere: there is no calculating the distance through which the stories come to us, the number of languages through which they have been filtered, or the centuries during which they have been told. Many of them have been narrated, almost in their present shape, for thousands of years since, to little copper-coloured Sanscrit children, listening to their mother under the palm-trees by the banks of the yellow Jumna—their Brahmin mother, who softly narrated them through the ring in her nose. The very same tale has been heard by the Northmen Vikings as they lay on their shields on deck; and by Arabs couched under the stars on the Syrian plains when the flocks were gathered in and the mares were picketed by the tents. With regard to the story of Cinderella, I have heard the late Thomas Hill say that he remembered to have heard, two years before Richard Cœur de Lion came back from Palestine, a Norman jongleur—but, in a word, there is no end to the antiquity of these tales...."—"Michael Angelo Titmarsh on Some Illustrated Children's Books," in *Fraser's Magazine* for April, 1846.

I. HORN-BOOKS; CHAP-BOOKS; THE NEW ENGLAND PRIMER.

Previous to the impetus given to child study by the educational theories of Rousseau, little was written intentionally for children that would not at the same time appeal to adults. Yet there are chapters still to be penned, stretching back into English history as far as 1430 and earlier, when words of instruction were framed for youth; when conduct, formality, austere manners, complete submission, were not only becoming to the child, but were forced upon him.[15]

There are several manuscripts extant of that year, 1430, one whose authorship is ascribed to John Lydgate and which bears the Latin title, "Puer ad Mensam." There is also the "Babees Book" of 1475, intended for those boys of royal blood who served as pages in the palace. The American student has to reach an understanding of the purport of most of these treatises from secondary sources; the manuscripts are not easily accessible, and have so far been utilised only in a fragmentary character. For the present purpose, the mention of a few examples will suffice.

We note "A Booke in Englyssh metre, of the great marchaunt man called Dyves Pragmaticus, very pretye for chyldren to rede; wherby they may the better, and more readyer rede and wryte Wares and Implementes in this worlde contayned.... When thou sellest aught unto thy neighbour, or byest anything of him, deceave not, nor oppresse him, etc. Imprinted at London in Aldersgate strete by Alexander Lacy, dwellyng beside the Wall. The XXV. of April 11, 1563."[16]

Those boys bound out or apprenticed to members of the Middle Age crafts and guilds perhaps benefited by the moral of this; no doubt they bethought themselves of the friendly warning, whenever they cried their master's wares outside the stalls; perhaps they were forearmed as well as forewarned by the friendly rules contained in the "Books of Good Manners" (1560) which, though they could not own, were repeated to them by others more fortunate. These same boys, who played the angels in the miracle plays, and the Innocents in the "Rachel" dramas, who were held suspended by a rope high up in the nave of the church, to proclaim the birth of the Lord in the Christmas cycles, were actors also, around 1563, in "A New Enterlude for Chyldren to Play, named Jacke Jugeler, both wytte, and very playsent."

Fundamentally, the boys of the early centuries must have been not unlike the boys of all ages, although the customs of an age usually stunt whatever is not in conformity with the times. He who, in 1572, was warned in "Youth's Behaviour" ("or, Decency in Conversation Amongst Men, Composed in French by Grave Persons, for the use and benefit of their youth, now newly turned into English, by Francis Hawkins, nephew to Sir Thomas Hawkins. The tenth impression."), was likewise warned in the New-England township, and needs to be warned to-day. No necessity to paint the picture in more definite colours than those emanating from the mandates direct. "Hearing thy Master, or likewise the Preacher, wriggle not thyself, as seeming unable to contain thyself within thy skin." Uncomfortable in frills or stiff collars, and given no backs to benches, the child was doomed to a dreary sermon full of brimstone and fire; he was expected, "in yawning, [to] howl not." The translation, it will be remarked, was made by Master Francis when he had scarce attained the age of eight; this may be considered precocious, but, when French was more the official language than English, it was necessary that all persons of any distinction should have a mastery of the polite tongue, even though they might remain not so well equipped in the language of learning.[17] Hawkins was therefore carefully exercised and the translation became a task in a twofold way. His uncle soon followed the first section of "Youth's Behaviour" with a second part, intended for girls.

Poor starved souls of those young gentlewomen of the sixteenth century, who were recommended, for their entertainment in hours of recreation, to read "God's Revenge against Murther; and the Arcadia of Sir Philip Sydney; Artemidorus, his Interpretation of Dreams. And for the business of their devotion, there is an excellent book entitled Taylor's Holy Living and Dying; The Duty of Man in which the Duty to God and man are both comprehended." Such guidance is not peculiar alone to this period. It was followed, in slightly simplified form, throughout the didactic school of writing.

Fortunately we are able, by means of our historical imagination, to fill up the interstices of this grave assemblage with something of a more entertaining character; we have a right to include the folk tales, the local legends and hero deeds which have descended to us through countless telling. Romance and interest still lie buried in annals which might be gathered together, dealing with the lives of those nurses who reared ancient kings. As a factor in the early period of children's literature, the grandam is of vast meaning.

About the time of which we have just been speaking, as early as 1570, little folks began learning their letters from horn-books and "battle-dores." Take an abacus frame and transfer the handle to one of its sides as a base. Within the frame insert a single leaf of thick cardboard, on one side of which place the alphabet, large and small, lettered heavily in black. Then, with the regularity of a regiment, string out three or four slender columns of monosyllables. Do we not here detect the faint glimmer of our college song, "b-a, ba; b-e, be; b-i, bi; babebi"? Should one side not hold all this, use both, although it is not preferable to do so. However, it *is* essential that ample room be left in any case for the inclusion of the Lord's Prayer. When this is done, slip over the face of the cardboard a clear piece of diaphanous horn, in default of which isinglass will suffice. Through the handle bore a hole, into which run a string. Finally, attach your handiwork to a girdle or belt, and behold, you are transformed into a school child of the Middle Ages! Your abacus has become a horn-book, quite as much by reason of its horn surface, as because of its essential use. Should you be looking for historical accuracy, let the "Christ-cross" precede the alphabet, whence it will become apparent why our letters are often styled the Criss-cross row. Flourishing until some time during the reign of George II, these curiosities are now rare indeed. There is little of an attractive nature in such a "lesson-book," but childhood had its compensations, for there is preserved the cheerful news that horn-books were often made of gingerbread. Were these the forebears of our animal crackers or our spiced alphabets?

A survey of chap-books[18] presents a picture of literature trying to be popular; we find all classes of people being catered to, young and old, rich and poor. The multitude of assorted pamphlets reflects the manners, the superstitions, the popular customs of rustics; the stories stretch from the humourous to the strictly religious type. There are many examples preserved, for not until well on in the nineteenth century were chap-books supplanted in favour. To-day, the largest collection that the world possesses, garnered by Professor Child, is to be found in the Harvard University Library; but the Bodleian and the British Museum claim to be richer in early examples, extending back to 1598.

Charles Gerring, calling the chap-books "uninviting, poor, starved things," yet lays before readers not an unwholesome array of goods. He writes:

"For the lads, there were tales of action, of adventure, sometimes truculently sensational; for the girls were stories of a more domestic character; for the tradesmen, there was the 'King and the Cobbler,' or 'Long Tom the Carrier'; for the soldier and the sailor, 'Admiral Blake,' 'Johnny Armstrong,' and 'Chevy Chase'; for the lovers, 'Patient Grissil' and 'Delights for Young Men and Maids'; for the serving-lad, 'Tom Hickathrift'[19] and 'Sir Richard Whittington'; while the serving-maid then, as now, would prefer 'The Egyptian Fortune Teller,' or 'The Interpretation of Dreams and Moles.'"

Every phase of human nature was thus served up for a penny. In those days, people were more apt to want tales with heroes and heroines of their own rank and station; a certain appropriateness in this way was satisfied. Such correspondence was common as early as 1415, when a mystery play was presented by the crafts, and the Plasterers were given the "Creation of the World" to depict, while the Chandlers were assigned the "Lighting of the Star" upon the birth of Christ.

There were to be had primers, song-books, and joke-books; histories, stories, and hero tales. Printed in type to ruin eyes, pictured in wood-cuts to startle fancy and to shock taste—for they were not always suited to childhood—these pamphlets, 2½" × 3½", sometimes 5½" × 4¼" in size, and composed of from four to twenty-four pages, served a useful purpose. They placed literature within reach of all who could read. Queer dreams, piety of a pronounced nature, jests with a ribald meaning, and riddles comprised the content of many of them. A child who could not buy a horn-book turned to the "battle-dore" with his penny—a crude sheet of cardboard, bicoloured and folded either once or twice, with printing on both sides; the reading matter was never-failingly the same in these horn-books and "battle-dores," although sometimes the wood-cuts varied. A horn-book is recorded with a picture of Charles I upon it.

The sixteenth or seventeenth-century boy could own his "Jack and the Giants" and "Guy of Warwick," his "Hector of Troy" and "Hercules of Greece"; he could even have the latest imported novelty. Some believe that because Shakespeare based many of his plays upon Continental legends, a demand was started for such chap-books as "Fortunatus," "Titus Andronicus," or "Valentine and Orson." The printers of these crude booklets were on the alert for every form of writing having a popular appeal; there was rivalry among them as there is rivalry among publishers to-day. Not long after the appearance of the English translation of Perrault's "Tales of Mother Goose," each one of them, given a separate and attractive form— "Blue-beard" in awful ferocity, "Cinderella" in gorgeous apparel, and the others—was made into a chap-book. In Ashton, we find mention of an early catalogue "of Maps, Prints, Copy-books, Drawing-books, Histories, Old Ballads, Patters, Collections, etc., printed and sold by Cluer Dicey and Richard Marshall at the Printing-Office in Aldermary (4) Church Yard, London. Printed in the year MDCCLXIV." These men appear to have been important chap-book publishers.

The hawkers, who went through the streets and who travelled the countryside, much as our pioneer traders were accustomed to do, were termed chapmen. They were eloquent in the manner of describing their display; they were zealous as to their line of trade. Imagine, if you will, the scene in some isolated village—the wild excitement when the good man arrived. He was known to Piers Plowman in 1362, he perhaps wandered not far away from the Canterbury Pilgrims; each of Chaucer's Tales might well be fashioned as a chap-book. Along the dusty highway this old-time peddler travelled, with packet on his back and a stout staff in hand—such a character maybe as Dougal Grahame, hunch-backed and cross-eyed—by professions, a town crier and bellman, as well as a trader in literature. On his tongue's tip he carried the latest gossip; he served as an instrument of cross-fertilisation, bringing London-town in touch with Edinburgh or Glasgow, and with small hamlets on the way.

"Do you wish to know, my lady," he would ask, "how fares the weather on the morrow?" From the depths of his packet he would draw "The Shepherd's Prognostication" (1673), wherein is told that "the blust'ring and noise of leaves and trees and woods, or *other places* is a token of foul weather." "And prithee, mistress," he would add, "I have a warning herein for you. A mole on the forehead denotes fair riches, but yonder brown spot on your eyebrow bids me tell you to refrain from marriage, for if he marry you, he shall have seven wives in his life-time!"

Many a modern reader would be interested in the detailed directions given for falling in love and for falling out again; for determining whom fate had decreed as the husband, or who was to be the wife. It is more wholesome in these days to name the four corners of a bedroom than to submit to the charm of a pared onion, wrapped in a kerchief and placed on the pillow; yet the two methods must be related.

For the little ones, there were picture-books in bright colours, smug in their anachronisms. The manufacturers of chap-books never hesitated to use the same wood-cuts over and over again; Queen Anne might figure in a history, but she served as well in the capacity of Sleeping Beauty; more appropriate in its historical application seems to have been the appearance of Henry VIII as Jack the Giant-Killer.

The subject of chap-books is alluring; the few elements here noted suggest how rich in local colour the material is. Undoubtedly the roots of juvenile literature are firmly twined about these penny sheets. Their circulation is a matter that brings the social student in touch with the middle-class life. Not only the chap-books and the horn-books, but the so-called Garlands, rudimentary anthologies of popular poems and spirited ballads, served to relieve the drudgery of commonplace lives, toned the sluggish mind by quickening the imagination. A curious part of the history of these Garlands is their sudden disappearance, brought about by two types of hawkers, known as the "Primers-up" and "Long-Song Sellers," who peddled a new kind of ware.

The Primers-up are relatives of our city venders. They clung to corners, where dead walls gave them opportunity to pin their literature within sight of the public. Wherever there happened to be an unoccupied house, one of these fellows would be found with his songs, coarse, sentimental, and spirited, cut in slips a yard long—three yards for a penny. Thus displayed, he would next open a gaudy umbrella, upon the under side of which an art gallery of cheap prints was free to look upon. Conjure up for yourselves the apprentice peering beneath the large circumference of such a gingham tent.

Across the way, the Long-Song Sellers marched up and down, holding aloft stout poles, from which streamed varied ribbons of verse—rhythm fluttering in the breeze—and yelling, "Three yards a penny, songs, beautiful songs, nooest songs."

It is apparent that much of the horn-book is incorporated in the "New England Primer," although the development of the latter may be considered independently. The Primer is an indispensable part of Puritan history in America, despite the fact that its source extends as far back as the time of Henry VIII, when it was probably regarded more in the light of a devotional than of an educational book. The earliest mention of it in New England was that published in the Boston *Almanac* of 1691, when Benjamin Harris, bookseller and printer, called attention to its second impression.[20] Before that, in 1685, Samuel Green, a Boston printer, issued a primer which he called "The Protestant Teacher for Children," and a copy of which may be seen in the library of the American Antiquarian Society of Worcester, Massachusetts. The title would indicate also that in America the primer for children at first served the same purpose as the morality play for adults in England; it was a vehicle for religious instruction.

The oldest existent copy of the New England Primer bears the imprint of Thomas Fleet, son-in-law of the famous Mrs. Goose, of whom we shall speak later. This was in 1737. Before then, in 1708, Benjamin Eliot of Boston, probably encouraged by earlier editions of primers, advertised "The First Book for Children; or, The Compleat School-Mistress"; and Timothy Green in 1715 announced "A Primer for the Colony of Connecticut; or, an Introduction to the True Reading of English. To which is added Milk for Babes." This latter title suggests the name of the Reverend John Cotton, and, furthermore, the name of Cotton Mather, one of the austere writers, as the titles of his books alone bear witness.

Six copies of the New England Primer lay before me, brown paper covers, dry with age; blue boards, worn with much handling; others in gray and green that have faded like the age which gave them birth. The boy who brought them to me wore a broad smile upon his face; perhaps he was wondering why I wished such toy books, no larger than $3¼" \times 2½"$. He held them all in one hand so as to show his superior strength. Yet had he been taken into the dark corridor between the book stacks, and had he been shown the contents of those crinkly leaves, there might have crept over him some remnant of the feeling of awe which must have seized the Colonial boy and girl. What would he have thought of the dutiful child's promises, or of the moral precepts, had they been read to him? Would he have shrunk backward at the description of the bad boy? Would he have beamed with youthful hope of salvation upon the picture of the good boy? It is doubtful whether the naughty girls, called "hussies," ever reformed; it is doubtful whether they ever wanted to be the good girl of the verses. That smiling boy of the present would have turned grave over the cut of Mr. John Rogers in the flames, despite the placid expression of wonderful patience over the martyr's face; his knees would have trembled at the sombre meaning of the lines:

"I in the burial place may see

Graves shorter far than I;

From death's arrest no age is free,

Young children too may die."

The New England Primers[21] were called pleasant guides; they taught that the longest life is a lingering death. There was the fear instead of the love of God in the text, and yet the type of manhood fostered by such teaching was no wavering type, no half-way spirit. The Puritan travelled the narrow road, but he faced it, however dark the consequences.

Sufficient has been said to give some idea of the part occupied by these early publications—whether horn-book, chap-book, or primer. They bore an intimate relation to the life of the child; they were, together with the Almanack, which is typified by that of "Poor Richard," and with the Calendar, part of a development which may be traced, with equal profit, in England, Scotland, France, and Germany. Their full history is fraught with human significance.

II. La Fontaine and Perrault.

Folk-lore stretches into the Valhalla of the past; our heritage consists of an assemblage of the heroic through all ages. A history of distinctive books for children must enter into minute traceries of the golden thread of legend, fable, and belief, of romance and adventure; it must tell of the wanderings of rhyme and marvel, under varied disguises, from mouth to mouth, from country to country, naught of richness being taken away from them, much of new glory being added. But for our immediate purposes, we imagine all this to be so; we take it for granted that courtier and peasant have had their fancies. The tales told to warriors are told to children, and in turn by nurses to these children's children. The knight makes his story by his own action in the dark forest, or in the king's palace; he appears before the hut of the serf, and his horse is encircled by a magic light. The immortal hero is kept immortal by what is heroic in ourselves.

Jean de La Fontaine (1621–1695) was a product of court life; and the fable was the literary form introduced to amuse the corsaged ladies of Versailles. La Fontaine was the cynic in an age of hypocrisy and favouritism, and one cannot estimate his work fully, apart from the social conditions fostering it. He was steeped in French lore, and in a knowledge of the popular tales of the Middle Ages. He was licentious in some of his writing, and wild in his living; he was a friend of Fouquet, and he knew Molière, Racine, and Boileau. He was a brilliant, unpractical satirist, who had to be supported by his friends, and who was elected to the Academy because his monarch announced publicly that he had promised to behave. Toward the end of his life he atoned for his misdemeanours by a formal confession.

There was much of the child heart in La Fontaine, and this characteristic, together with the spleen which develops in every courtier, aided him in his composition of the Fables. Unclean his tales may be, likened to Boccaccio, but the true poet in him produced incomparable verses which have been saved for the present and will live far into the future because of the universality of their moral. The wolf and dog, the grasshopper and ant, all moved in silks and satins at the court of Louis XIV, and bowed for social rank, some trailing their pride in the dust, others raised to high position through the fortune of unworthy favour. So successfully did La Fontaine paint his pictures that the veiled allusions became lost in time beneath the distinct individuality of the courtiers' animal prototypes. The universal in La Fontaine is like the universal in Molière and Shakespeare, but it has a wider appeal, for children relish it as their own.

Another figure was dominant at the court of Louis XIV—one equally as immortal as La Fontaine, though not so generally known—Charles Perrault (1628–1703). He was a brilliant genius, versatile in talent and genial in temper. He dabbled in law, he dabbled in architecture, and through it won the favour of Colbert. With an abiding love for children, he suggested and successfully carried the idea of keeping open the royal gardens for young Parisians. Through Colbert he became an Academician in 1671, and, with the energy which usually marked his actions, he set about influencing the rulings of that body. He was a man of progress, not an advocate of classical formalism. He battled long and hard with Boileau, who was foremost among the Classicists; his appeal was for the future rather than for the past. He was intellectually alert in all matters; probably, knowing that he possessed considerable hold upon the Academy, he purposely startled that august gathering by his statement that had Homer lived in the days of Louis XIV he would have made a better poet. But the declaration was like a burning torch set to dry wood; Boileau blazed forth, and the fight between himself and Perrault, lasting some time, became one of the most famous literary quarrels that mark the pages of history.

After Perrault retired to his home in the year 1686, and when he could have his children around him, he began the work which was destined to last. Lang calls him "a good man, a good father, a good Christian, and a good fellow." It is in the capacity of father that we like to view him—taking an interest in the education of his children, listening to them tell their tales which they had first heard from their nurse; his heart became warmed by their frank, free *camaraderie*, and it is likely that these impromptu story hours awakened in him some dim memories of the same legends told him in his boyhood.

There is interesting speculation associated with his writing of the "Contes de ma Mère l'Oye." They were published in 1697, although previously they had appeared singly in Moetjen's Magazine at the Hague. An early letter from Madame de Sévigné mentions the wide-spread delight taken by the nobles of the court in all "contes"; this was some twenty years before Perrault penned his. But despite their popularity among the worldly wise, the Academician was too much of an Academician to confess openly that he was the author of the "contes." Instead, he ascribed them to his son, Perrault Darmancour. This has raised considerable doubt among scholars as to whether the boy should really be held responsible for the authorship of the book. Mr. Lang wisely infers that there is much evidence throughout the tales of the mature feeling and art of Perrault; but he also is content to hold to the theory that will blend the effort of old age and youth, of father and son.

The fact remains that, were it not for Perrault, the world might have been less rich by such immortal pieces as "The Three Wishes," "The Sleeping Beauty," "Red Riding Hood," "Blue Beard," "Puss in Boots," and "Cinderella," as they are known to us to-day. They might have reached us from other countries in modified form, but the inimitable pattern belongs to Perrault.

Another monument preserves his name, the discussion of which requires a section by itself. But consideration must be paid in passing to the "fées" of Marie Catherine Jumelle de Berneville, Comtesse D'Anois (Aulnoy) [1650 or 51–1705], who is responsible for such tales as "Finetta, the Cinder-Girl."[22] Fortunately, to the charm of her fairy stories, which are written in no mean imitation of Perrault, there have clung none of the qualities which made her one of the most intriguing women of her period. She herself possessed a magnetic personality and a bright wit. Her married life began at the age of sixteen, and through her career lovers flocked to her standard; because of the ardour of one, she came near losing her head. But despite the fact that only two out of five of her children could claim legitimacy, they seem to have developed in the Comtesse d'Aulnoy an unmistakable maternal instinct, and an unerring judgment in the narration of stories. She is familiar to-day because of her tales, although recently an attractive edition of her "Spanish Impressions" was issued—a book which once received the warm commendation of Taine.

III. MOTHER GOOSE.

There has been a sentimental desire on the part of many students to trace the origin of Mother Goose to this country; but despite all effort to the contrary, and a false identification of Thomas Fleet's mother-in-law, Mrs. Goose, or Vergoose, with the famous old woman, the origin is indubitably French. William H. Whitmore[23] sums up his evidence in the matter as follows:

"According to my present knowledge, I feel sure that the original name is merely a translation from the French; that the collection was first made for and by John Newbery of London, about A.D. 1760; and that the great popularity of the book is due to the Boston editions of Munroe and Francis, A.D. 1824–1860."

It appears that, in 1870, William A. Wheeler edited an edition of "Mother Goose," wherein he averred that Elizabeth, widow of one Isaac Vergoose, was the sole originator of the jingles. This statement was based upon the assurances of a descendant, John Fleet Eliot. But there is much stronger evidence in Perrault's favour than mere hearsay; even the statement that a 1719 volume of the melodies was printed by Fleet himself has so far failed of verification.

The name, Mother Goose, is first heard of in the seventeenth century. During 1697, Perrault published his "Histoires ou Contes du Tems Passé avec des Moralitez," with a frontispiece of an old woman telling stories to an interested group. Upon a placard by her side was lettered the significant title already quoted:

CONTES

DE MA

MERE

LOYE

There is no doubt, therefore, that the name was not of Boston origin; some would even go further back and mingle French legend with history; they would claim that the mother of Charlemagne, with the title of Queen Goose-foot (Reine Pédance), was the only true source.[24]

Mr. Austin Dobson has called Mr. Lang's attention to the fact that in the *Monthly Chronicle* for March, 1729, an English version of Perrault's "Tales" was mentioned, done by Mr. Robert Samber, and printed by J. Pote; another English edition appeared at The Hague in 1745. This seems to be the first introduction into England of the "Mother Goose Fairy Tales." It was probably their popularity, due not only to their intrinsic interest, but partly to the speculation as to Mother Goose's identification, that made John Newbery, the famous London publisher, conceive the brilliant plan of gathering together those little songs familiar to the nursery, and of laying them to the credit of Mother Goose herself. In so doing, he solicited the assistance of Oliver Goldsmith (1728–1774). Mr. Whitmore writes:

"If, as seems most probable, the first edition of 'Mother Goose's Melody' was issued prior to John Newbery's death in 1767, there is an interesting question as to who prepared the collection for the press. The rhymes are avowedly the favourites of the nursery, but the preface and the foot-notes are an evident burlesque upon more pretentious works."

There are two small pieces of evidence indicating clearly Goldsmith's editorship. On January 29, 1768, he produced his "Good Natur'd Man," and with his friends dined beforehand in gala fashion at an inn. Subject to extremes of humour, on this occasion he was most noisy, and he sang his favourite song, we are told, which was nothing more than "An old woman tossed in a blanket, seventeen times as high as the moon." As it happens, this ditty is mentioned in the preface to Newbery's collection of rhymes, without any more apparent reason than that it was a favourite with the editor, who wished to introduce it in some way, however irrelevant. Again, we are assured that Miss Hawkins once exclaimed, "I little thought what I should have to boast, when Goldsmith taught me to play Jack and Jill, by two bits of paper on his fingers."

Thus, though the tasks performed by Goldsmith for Newbery are generally accounted specimens of hack work, which he had to do in order to eke out a livelihood, there is satisfaction in claiming for him two immortal strokes, his tale of "Goody Two Shoes," and his share in the establishment of the Mother Goose Melodies.[25] Many a time he was dependent upon the beneficence of his publisher, many a time rescued by him from the hands of the bailiff. The Newbery accounts are dotted with entries of various loans; even the proceeds of the first performances of the "Good Natur'd Man" were handed over to Newbery to satisfy one of his claims.

The notes accompanying the melodies, and which have no bearing upon the child-interest in the collection, show a wit that might very well belong to Goldsmith. He was perhaps amusing himself at the expense of his lexicographer friend, Johnson. For instance, to the jingle, "See saw, Margery Daw," is appended this, taken seemingly from "Grotius": "It is a mean and scandalous Practice in Authors to put Notes to Things that deserve no Notice." And to the edifying and logical song, "I wou'd, if I cou'd, If I cou'dn't, how cou'd I? I cou'dn't, without I cou'd, cou'd I?" is attached the evident explanation from "Sanderson": "This is a new Way of handling an old Argument, said to be invented by a famous Senator; but it has something in it of *Gothick* Construction." Assuredly the names of those learned authors, "Mope," credited with the "Geography of the Mind," and "Huggleford," writing on "Hunger," were intended for ridicule.

By 1777, "Mother Goose" had passed into its seventh edition, but, though its success was largely assured, there are still to be noted rival publications. For instance, John Marshall,[26] who later became the publisher of Mrs. Trimmer's works, issued some rhymes, conflicting with the book of Melodies which Carnan, Newbery's stepson, had copyrighted in 1780, and had graced with a subtitle, "Sonnets for the Cradle." During 1842, J. O. Halliwell edited for the Percy Society, "The Nursery Rhymes of England, collected principally from Oral Tradition," and he mentioned an octavo volume printed in London, 1797, and containing some of our well-known verses. These it seems had been first collected by the scholar, Joseph Ritson,[27] and called "Gammer Gurton's Garland." The 1797 book was called "Infant Institutes," semi-satirical in its general plan, and was ascribed to the Reverend Baptist Noel Turner, M.A.,[28] rector of Denton. If this was intended to supplant Newbery's collection, it failed in its object. However, it is to be noted and emphasised that so varied did the editions become, that the fate of "Mother Goose" would not have been at all fortunate in the end, had not Monroe and Francis in Boston insisted upon the original collection as the authentic version, *circa* 1824. Its rights were thus established in America.

The melodies have a circuitous literary history. In roundabout fashion, the ditties have come out of the obscure past and have been fixed at various times by editors of zealous nature. For the folk-lore student, such investigation has its fascination; but the original rhymes are not all pure food for the nursery. In the course of time, the juvenile volumes have lost the jingles with a tang of common wit. They come to us now, gay with coloured print, rippling with merriment, with a rhythm that must be kept time to by a tap of the foot upon the floor or by some bodily motion. Claim for them, as you will, an educational value; they are the child's first entrance into storyland; they train his ear, they awaken his mind, they develop his sense of play. It is a joyous garden of incongruity we are bequeathed in "Mother Goose."

IV. JOHN NEWBERY, OLIVER GOLDSMITH, AND ISAIAH THOMAS.

Wherever you wander in the land of children's books, ramifications, with the vein of hidden gold, invite investigation,—rich gold for the student and for the critic, but less so for the general reader. Yet upon the general reader a book's immortality depends. No librarian, no historian, need be crowded out; there are points still to be settled, not in the mere dry discussion of dates, but in the estimates of individual effect. The development of children's books is consecutive, carried forward because of social reasons; each name mentioned has a story of its own. Two publishers at the outset attract our regard; except for them, much would have been lost to English and American children.

As early as Elizabeth's time, Rafe Newberie, Master of Stationer's Company, published Hakluyt's "Voyages." From him, John Newbery (1713–1767) was descended. Given an ordinary schooling, he was apprenticed to the printer, William Carnan, who, dying in 1737, divided his worldly goods between his brother Charles, and his assistant John. The latter, in order to cement his claim still further, married his employer's widow, by whom he had three children, Francis, his successor in the publishing business, being born on July 6, 1743.

Newbery was endowed with much common sense. He travelled somewhat extensively before settling in London, and, during his wanderings, he jotted down rough notes, relating especially to his future book trade; the remarks are worthy of a keen critic. During this time it is hard to keep Newbery, the publisher, quite free from the picturesque career of Newbery, the druggist; on the one hand Goldsmith might call him "the philanthropic publisher of St. Paul's Churchyard," as he did in the "Vicar of Wakefield," which was first printed by Newbery and Benjamin Collins, of Salisbury; on the other hand, in 1743, one might just as well have praised him for the efficacy of the pills and powders he bartered. Now we find him a shopkeeper, catering to the captains of ships from his warehouse, and adding every new concoction to his stock of homeopathic deceptions. Even Goldsmith could not refrain from having a slap at his friend in "Quacks Ridiculed."

He made money, however, and he associated with a literary set among whom gold was much coveted and universally scarce. The portly Dr. Johnson ofttimes borrowed a much-needed guinea, an unfortunate privilege, for he had a habit of never working so long as he could feel money in his pocket. This generosity on the part of Newbery did not deter Johnson from showing his disapproval over many of the former's publications. We can well imagine the implied sarcasm in his declaration that Newbery was an extraordinary man, "for I know not whether he has read, or written most books." Between 1744 and 1802, records indicate that Newbery and his successors printed some three hundred volumes, two hundred of which were juvenile; small wonder he needed the editorial assistance of such persons as Dr. Johnson and Oliver Goldsmith.

One of the first pieces the latter let Newbery have, was an article for the *Literary Magazine* of January, 1758. Then there came into existence *The Universal Chronicle, or Weekly Gazette* in April, 1758, for which Johnson wrote "The Idler." In 1759, *The British Magazine or Monthly Repository for Gentlemen and Ladies, by T. Smollett, M.D., and others* was announced, Smollett then taking a rest cure in jail. As though magazines could be launched in a few hours without sinking, a daily sheet called the *Public Ledger* was brought into existence on January 12, 1760, for which Goldsmith wrote his "Chinese Letters." Between this date and 1767, Goldsmith resided in a room on the upper floor of Newbery's house at Islington, and the publisher's son declares that while there Goldsmith read to him odd parts of "The Traveller" and the "Vicar of Wakefield." This has not so much evidence to support it as the fact that bills presented at the front door for Goldsmith, usually found their way to Newbery for settlement.

How much actual suggestion Goldsmith gave to his publisher-employer, how far he influenced the character of the books to be printed, cannot be determined; he and Griffith and Giles Jones assuredly encouraged the juvenile picture stories. An advertisement of 1765 calls attention to the following: "The Renowned History of Giles Gingerbread, a little boy who lived upon learning" [the combination is very appropriate in its compensating qualities of knowledge and "sweets"]; "The Whitsuntide Gift, or the Way to be Happy"; "The Valentine Gift, or how to behave with honour, integrity and humanity"; and "The History of Little Goody Two Shoes, otherwise called Margery Two Shoes."

Though he could not wholly escape the charge of catering to the moral craze of the time, Newbery at least infused into his little books something of imagination and something of heroic adventure; not sufficient however to please Dr. Johnson, who once said: "Babies do not want to hear about babies; they like to be told of giants and castles, and of somewhat which can stretch and stimulate their little minds." A thrust at the ignorance of grown people, regarding what children like, is further seen in Johnson's remark that parents buy, but girls and boys seldom read what is calculated for them.

There are many to praise Newbery's prints; they were more or less oddities, even in their own time. Their usefulness was typified in such books as the "Circle of Sciences," a compendium of universal knowledge; their attractiveness was dependent not only upon the beauty of their make, but also upon the queerness of their *format*; for example, such volumes as were called the snuff-box series, or ready references for waistcoat pockets. Then there was the combination plan, indicated in the announcement: "A Little Pretty Pocket-Book, intended for the Instruction and Amusement of Little Master Tommy and Pretty Miss Polly, with an agreeable letter to read from Jack-the-Giant-Killer, as also a Ball and Pincushion, the use of which will infallibly make Tommy a Good Boy, and Polly a Good Girl.... Price of the Book alone, 6d., with a Ball or Pincushion, 8d."

The variety of Newbery's ideas resulted in every species of book-publishing, from a children's magazine (*The Lilliputian*), with Goldsmith as the reputed editor, to a child's grammar. Interested one moment in a machine for the colouring of silks and cloths, at another he would be extolling the fever powders of Dr. James, a whilom schoolfellow of Johnson. He was untiring in his business activity. His firm changed name many times, but always Newbery remained the dominant figure. After his death, the business continued for some while to be identified with its founder, and for a long period his original policy was continued. Francis Newbery, the son, left an autobiography of historic value.

Newbery's real genius consisted in his trading ability. Modern advertising is not more clever than that practised by this shrewd man of the eighteenth century. Not only was he in the habit of soliciting puffs, and of making some of the characters in his stories proclaim the excellencies of his books, but the personal note and the friendly feeling displayed in his newspaper items were uncommonly intimate. Witness the London *Chronicle* for December 19–January 1, 1765:

"The Philosophers, Politicians, Necromancers, and the learned in every faculty are desired to observe that on the first of January, being New Year's day (oh, that we all may lead new lives!), Mr. Newbery intends to publish the following important volumes, bound and gilt, and hereby invites all his little friends who are good to call for them at the Bible and Sun, in St. Paul's Churchyard, but those who are naughty to have none."

Thomas in later years adopted the same method of advertising.

The most thorough piece of research work done by Mr. Charles Welsh is his "A Bookseller of the Last Century." Had he aimed at nothing more than preserving the catalogue of Newbery's books, he would have rendered a great service to the library student. But he has in addition written a very complete life of Newbery. When it is noted that this printer was brought into business relations with Robert Raikes, and was further connected with him by the union of Newbery's son with Raikes' sister, it is safe to believe that some of the piousness which crept into the publisher's wares was encouraged by the zealous spirit of the founder of Sunday-schools. Raikes will be dealt with in his proper place.

Newbery was what may be termed an enthusiastic publisher, a careful manufacturer of books of the flower-and-gilt species. As a friend he has been pictured nothing loath to help the needy, but always with generous security and heavy interest attached; he was a business man above all else, and that betokens keenness for a bargain, a keenness akin to cleverness rather than to graciousness. In his "Life of Goldsmith," Washington Irving is inclined to be severe in his estimate; he writes:

"The poet [Goldsmith] has celebrated him as the friend of all mankind; he certainly lost nothing by his friendship. He coined the brains of authors in the times of their exigency, and made them pay dear for the plank put out to keep them from drowning. It is not likely his death caused much lamentation among the scribbling tribe."

One difficulty Newbery had to contend with was the piracy of his books; there was no adequate protection afforded by the copyright system, and we read of Goldsmith and Johnson bewailing the literary thievery of the day. By some it was regarded as a custom to be accepted; by others as a deplorable condition beyond control. Early American authorship suffered from the same evil, and Irving and Cooper were the two prominent victims.

The book list of Isaiah Thomas (1749–1831), the Worcester, Massachusetts printer, shows how freely he drew from the London bookseller. Called by many the Didot of America, founder of the American Antiquarian Society, author of one of the most authentic histories of early printing in this country, he is the pioneer of children's books for America. He scattered his presses and stores over a region embracing Worcester and Boston, Mass.; Concord, N. H.; Baltimore, Md.; and Albany, N. Y. Books were kept by him, so he vouched, specially for the instruction and amusement of children, to make them safe and happy. In his "Memoirs" there is found abundant material to satisfy one as to the nature of reading for young folks in New England, previous to the Revolution.

Emerson writes in his "Spiritual Laws" regarding "theological problems"; he calls them "the soul's mumps and measles and whooping-cough." Already the sombre sternness of Colonial literature for children has been typified in the "New England Primer." The benefits of divine songs and praises; the reiteration of the joy to parents, consequent upon the behaviour of godly children; the mandates, the terrible finger of retribution, the warning to all sinners lurking in the throat disease which was prevalent at one time—all these ogres rise up in the Thomas book to crush juvenile exuberance. Does it take much description to get at the miserable heart of the early piety displayed by the heroines of Cotton Mather's volumes, those stone images of unthinkable children who passed away early, who were reclaimed from disobedience, "children in whom the fear of God was remarkably budding before they died"? Writers never fail to say, in speaking of Thomas White's "Little Book for Children" (reprint of 1702), that its immortality, in the face of all its theology, is centred in one famous untheological line, "A was an archer who shot at a frog."

What Thomas did, when he began taking from Newbery, was to change colloquial English terms to fit new environment; the coach no longer belongs to the Lord Mayor, but to the Governor instead.[29] The text is only slightly altered. We recognise the same little boys who would become great masters; the same ear-marks stigmatise the heroines of "The Juvenile Biographer," insufferable apostles of surname-meaning, Mistresses Allgood, Careful, and Lovebook, together with Mr. Badenough. Oh, Betsey and Nancy and Amelia and Billy, did you know what it was to romp and play?

The evident desire on the part of Miss Hewins, in her discussion of early juvenile books, to emphasise the playful, in her quotations from Thomas' stories, only indicates that there was little levity to deal with. Those were the days of gilded "Gifts" and "Delights"; the pleasures of childhood were strangely considered; goodness was inculcated by making the hair stand on end in fright, by picturing to the naughty boy what animal he was soon to turn into, and what foul beast's disposition was akin to that of the fractious girl. Intentions, both of an educational and religious nature, were excellent, no doubt; but, when all is estimated, the residue presents a miserable, lifeless ash.[30]

So far no distinctive writer for children has arisen. The volumes issued by Newbery represent a conscious attempt to appeal through *form* to the juvenile eye. If the books were addressed intentionally to children, their amusement consisted in some extraneous novelty; it was rarely contained in the story. Action rather than motive is the redeeming feature of "Goody Two Shoes." As for religious training, it was administered to the child with no regard for his individual needs. He represented a theological stage of sin; the world was a long dark road, through the maze of which, by his birth, he was doomed to fight his little way. Life was a probationary period.

It is now necessary to leave the New England book, and to return to it through another channel. The viewpoint shifts slightly; a new element is to be added: a self-conscious recognition of education for children. The sternness of the "New England Primer" possessed strength. The didactic school, retaining the moral factor,—several points removed from theology—sentimentalised it; for many a day it was to exist in juvenile literature rampant. And, overflowing its borders, it was to influence later chap-books, and some of the later publications of Thomas and Newbery. Through Hannah More, it was to grip Peter Parley, and finally to die out on American shores. For "Queechy" and "The Wide, Wide World" represent the final flowering of this style. In order to retain a clear connection, it is necessary to watch both streams, educational and moral, one at first blending with the other, and flourishing in this country through a long list of New England authors, until, in the end, the educational, increasing in volume, conquered altogether.

Bibliographical Note

THE BABEES BOOK—Ed. Frederick J. Furnivall, M.A. Published for the Early English Text Society. London, Trübner, 1868.

In the foreword, note the following:

Education in early England:

1. In Nobles' Houses; 2. At Home and at Private Tutors'; 3. At English Universities; 4. At Foreign Universities; 5. At Monastic and Cathedral Schools; 6. At Grammar Schools. *Vide* the several other prefaces.

This collection contains:

1. The Babees Book, or a 'Lytyl Reporte' of How Young People Should Behave (*circa* 1475 A.D.); 2. The A B C of Aristotle (1430 A.D.); 3. The Book of Curteisie That is Clepid Stans Puer ad Mensam (1430 A.D.); 4. The boke of Nurture, or Schoole of good maners: For Men, Servants, and children (1577); 5. The Schoole of Vertue, and booke of good Nourture for chyldren and youth to learne theyr dutie by (1557).

Vide Vol. iv, Percy Society, London, 1841:1. The Boke of Curtasye, ed. J. O. Halliwell. 2. Specimens of Old Christmas Carols, ed. T. Wright. 3. The Nursery Rhymes of England, ed. J. O. Halliwell, 1842: *a.* Historical; *b.* Tales; *c.* Jingles; *d.* Riddles; *e.* Proverbs; *f.* Lullabies; *g.* Charms; *h.* Games; *i.* Literal; *j.* Paradoxes; *k.* Scholastic; *l.* Customs; *m.* Songs; *n.* Fragments.

Vide Vol. xxix, Percy Society, London, 1849. Notices of Fugitive Tracts and Chap-books printed at Aldermary Churchyard, Bow Churchyard, etc., ed. J. O. Halliwell.

ASHTON, JOHN—Chap-books of the 18th Century.

ASHTON, JOHN—Social Life in the Time of Queen Anne.

BERGENGREN, R.—Boswell's Chap-books and Others. *Lamp*, 28:39–44 (Feb., 1904).

CHAMBERS, W.—Historical Sketch of Popular Literature and Its Influence on Society, 1863.

CUNNINGHAM, R. H.—Amusing Prose Chap-books. Glasgow, 1889.

FAXON, FREDERICK WINTHROP—A Bibliography of the Modern Chap-books and their Imitators (Bulletin of Bibl. Pamphl. No. 11), Boston Book Co., 1903. [A "freak" movement, beginning with the publication of *Chap-book*, at Cambridge, May 15, 1894.]

FERGUSON, CHANCELLOR—On the Chap-books in the Bibliotheca Jacksoniana in Tullie House, Carlisle. *Archaeol. Jour.*, 52:292 (1895).

FRASER, JOHN—Scottish Chap-books. (2 pts.) New York, Hinton, 1873.

GERRING, CHARLES—Notes on Printers and Booksellers, with a Chapter on Chap-books. London, 1900.

HALLIWELL, JAMES ORCHARD—A Catalogue of Chap-books, Garlands, and Popular Histories in the Possession of Halliwell. London, 1849.

HARVARD COLLEGE LIBRARY—Catalogue of English and American Chap-books and Broadside Ballads in 1905 (Bibl. contrib. No. 56).

NISARD, MARIE LÉONARD CHARLES—Histoire des Livres Populaires ou de la Littérature du Colportage, depuis l'origine de l'imprimerie jusqu' à l'établissement de la Commission d'examen des livres du Colportage (30 Nov., 1852) [2 vols.]. Paris, Dentu, 1864.

PEARSON, EDWIN—Banbury Chap-books and Nursery Toy Book Literature of the 18th and Early 19th Centuries. London, 1890.

PYLE, HOWARD—Chap-book Heroes. *Harper's Monthly Magazine*, 81:123 (1890).

SIEVEKING, S. GIBERNE—The Mediæval Chap-book as an Educational Factor in the Past. *The Reliquary and Illus. Archaeolog.*, 9:241 (1903).

The student is referred to the following invaluable reference for matter relating to New England literature: Catalogue of the American Library of the Late Mr. George Brinley of Hartford, Conn. (5 pts.) Hartford: Press of the Case, Lockwood, and Brainard Co., 1878–97. Not completed. Comprising a list of Books printed at Cambridge and Boston, 1640–1709.

Pt. I.—The Bay Psalm Book, No. 847; Almanacs, 1646–1707; The Mathers, Special Chapter of References.

Pt. III.—Bibles, 146; Catechisms and Primers, New England Primer, 158; Music and Psalmody, 163; Psalms and Hymns, 172.

Pt. IV.—Continuation of Psalms and Hymns; Bibl. Ref. to Denominational Churches, Law, Government, Political Economy, Sciences, etc.; Popular Literature: Jest Books, Anecdotes, 131; Chap-books, 135; Books for Children, 139; Mother Goose, 140; Primers and Catechisms, 141; Educational, 143; Almanacs, 163; Theology, 177.

Pt. V.—Newspapers and Periodicals, 137.

FORD, PAUL LEICESTER—The New England Primer (ed.). N. Y., Dodd, Mead, 1897. (Edition limited.) [*Vide* excellent bibliography.]

The New England Primer. *Bookman*, 4:122–131 (Oct., 1896).

JOHNSON, CLIFTON—The New England Primer. *New England Mag.*, n.s. 28:323. (May, 1903.) [Some essential data, but written superficially.]

MARBLE, ANNIE RUSSELL—Early New England Almanacs. *New England Mag.*, n.s. 19:548. (Jan., 1899.) [*Vide* also Griswold's Curiosities of American Literature; Tyler's History of American Literature; Thomas's History of Printing. A collection of Almanacs is owned by the Am. Antiq. Soc., Worcester, Mass.]

COLLIN DE PLANCY—Memories of Perrault.

DILLAYE, FRÉDÉRIC—Les Contes de Perrault (ed.). Paris, 1880.

LANG, ANDREW—Perrault's Popular Tales; edited from the original editions, with an introduction by. Oxford, Clarendon Press, 1888. [A concise and agreeable introduction to the study of folk-lore in general, and of a few noted tales in particular.]

OLD-FASHIONED FAIRY TALES—Madame D'Aulnoy, Charles Perrault, etc. Little, Brown, $1.00.

OLD FRENCH FAIRY TALES—C. Perrault, Madame D'Aulnoy. Little, Brown, $1.00.

D'ANOIS, COUNTESS—Fairy Tales, Translated from the French of. (2 vols.) London, 1817.

D'AULNOY, COMTESSE—Mémoires de la. [*Vide* Collection pour les jeunes filles.]

HALE, EDWARD EVERETT—Reprint of the Monroe and Francis Mother Goose.

GREEN, P. B.—History of Nursery Rhymes. London, 1899.

HEADLAND, J. T.—Chinese Mother Goose. Chicago, 1900.

HALLIWELL, J. O.—Nursery Rhymes of England; collected principally from oral tradition. London, 1842. [The Percy Society, Early English Poetry.]

Popular Rhymes and Nursery Tales. A Sequel to Nursery Rhymes. London, 1849.

RITSON, JOSEPH—Gammer Gurton's Garland; or, The Nursery Parnassus. London, 1810; reprint 1866.

WELSH, CHARLES—An Appeal for Nursery Rhymes and Jingles. *Dial* (Chicago), 27:230 (1 Oct., 1899).

FATHER OF CHILDREN'S BOOKS—*Current Literature*, 27:110.

WELSH, CHARLES—A Bookseller of the Last Century. Griffith, Farren & Co. London.

BATCHELDER, F. R.—Patriot Printer. *New England Mag.*, n.s. 25:284 (N. '01).

EVANS, CHARLES—American Bibliography. A Chronological Dictionary of all Books, Pamphlets, and Periodical Publications Printed in the United States of America. From the genesis of Printing in 1639 Down to and Including the Year 1820. With Bibliographical and Biographical Notes. Privately Printed for the Author by the Blakely Press, Chicago. Anno Domini

MDCCCCIII. Thus far issued: Vol. I. 1639–1729; Vol. II. 1730–1750; Vol. III. 1751–1764.

LIVINGSTON, L. S.—American Publisher of a Hundred Years Ago. *Bookman*, 11:530 (Aug., '00).

NICHOLS, CHARLES L.—Some Notes on Isaiah Thomas and his Worcester Imprints. *Am. Antiq. Soc.*, 1899–1900, n.s., 13:429.

THOMAS, BENJAMIN FRANKLIN—Memoir of Isaiah Thomas. By his Grandson. Boston, 1874.

HEWINS, CAROLINE M.—The History of Children's Books. *Atlantic*, 61:112 (Jan., 1888).

WELSH, CHARLES.—The Early History of Children's Books in New England. *New England Mag.*, n.s. 20:147–60 (April, 1899).

YONGE, CHARLOTTE M.—Children's Literature of the Last Century. *Liv. Age*, 102:373 (Aug. 7, 1869); 612 (Sept. 4, 1869); 103:96 (Oct. 9, 1869).

FOOTNOTES

[15] In "The Child and His Book," by Mrs. E. M. Field (London: Wells Gardner, Darton & Co., 1892), the reader is referred to chapters: Before the Norman Conquest; Books from the Conquest to Caxton; The Child in England, 1066–1640. Her researches form an invaluable contribution to the history of children's books, furnishing sources for considerable speculation. Much is included of interest to the antiquarian only.

[16] Thomas Newbery was the author. *Vide* Fugitive Tracts, 1875. Hazlitt and Huth.

[17] As early as 1262, the *macaronic* style of delivering sermons was customary. The gradual substitution of the vernacular for Latin is dealt with in the introduction to the present author's edition of "Everyman," 1903, xxvii.

[18] CHAP = An abbreviation of Chapman, which seems to have come into vulgar use in the end of the 16th c.; but it is rare in books, even in the dramatists, before 1700. It was not recognised by Johnson. 1577 BRETON *Toyes Idle* Head (Grosart). Those crusty chaps I cannot love. *a.* A buyer, purchaser, customer.

CHAP-BOOK = f. *chap* in Chapman + Book. A modern name applied by book collectors and others to specimens of the popular literature which was formerly circulated by itinerant dealers or chapmen, consisting chiefly of small pamphlets of popular tales, etc. 1824 DIBDIN *Libr. Comp.* It is a chapbook, printed in rather neat black letter. 1882 J. ASHTON *Chap-books, 18th Century* in *Athenæum* 2 Sept. 302/1. A great mass of chap-books.

CHAPMAN = [OE. Céapmann = OHG. Choufman (OHG., MHG. Koufman), Ger. Kaufmann.] A man whose business is buying and selling; a merchant, trader, dealer. *Vide* 890 K. ÆLFRED *Bæda*. *Vide* further, A New English Dictionary. Murray, Oxford.

[19] "The History of Tom Hickathrift" is regarded as distinctively English; its literary qualities were likened by Thackeray to Fielding. *Vide Fraser's Magazine.*

[20] The notice ran as follows: "Advertisement: There is now in the Press, and will suddenly be extant, a Second Impression of *The New England Primer, enlarged*, to which is added, more *Directions for Spelling*; the *Prayer of K. Edward the 6th*, and *Verses made by Mr. Rogers, the Martyr, left as a Legacy to his Children. Sold by Benjamin Harris*, at the *London Coffee-House* in *Boston.*"

[21] Three typical examples of later reprints are: The N. E. Primer, Walpole, N. H., I. Thomas & Co., 1814; The N. E. Primer Improved for the More Easy Attaining the True Reading of English. To which is added The Assembly of Divines and Episcopal Catechisms. N. Y., 1815; The N. E. Primer, or an Easy and Pleasant Guide to the Art of Reading, Mass. Sabbath School Soc., 1841.

[22] Another writer of *Contes des fées* was Mme. Jeanne Marie Le Prince de Beaumont (1711–1780), author of "Magasins des Enfans, des Adolescens et des Dames."

[23] The Original Mother Goose's Melody, as first issued by John Newbery, of London, about A.D. 1760. Reproduced in *facsimile* from the edition as reprinted by Isaiah Thomas, of Worcester, Mass., about A.D. 1785. With Introductory Notes by William H. Whitmore. Albany, Munsell, 1889. [*Vide* N. E. Hist. and Geneal. Regist., 1873, pp. 144, 311; Proceed. Am. Antiq. Soc., Oct., 1888, p. 406.]

[24] Lang says the term *Mother Goose* appears in Loret's "La Muse Historique" (Lettre v., 11 Juin, 1650). *Vide* also Deulin, Charles—Les Contes de Ma Mère L'Oye, avant Perrault. Paris, 1878; and Halliwell, J. O.—Percy Society.

[25] He was the author also of a "History of Animated Nature."

[26] A list of his publications is owned by the Bodleian Library, Oxford.

[27] *Vide Notes and Queries*, June, 1875, 5th series, iii, 441. Prof. Edward F. Rimbault.

[28] *Gentleman's Magazine*, 1826, Pt. ii, 467–69.

[29] Nurse Truelove's New Year's Gift; or, the Book of Books for Children. Adorned with Cuts; and designed for a Present to every little Boy who would become a great Man, and ride upon a fine Horse; and to every little Girl, who would become a great Woman, and ride in a Governour's Gilt Coach.

[30] An interesting field of investigation: Early New England Printers. Mr. Welsh mentions a few in article referred to, p.60. A full list of Printers and Publishers (North and South) given in Evans's American Bibliography.

III.
THE OLD-FASHIONED LIBRARY

A child should not need to choose between right and wrong. It should not be capable of wrong; it should not conceive of wrong. Obedient, as bark to helm, not by sudden strain or effort, but in the freedom of its bright course of constant life; true, with an undistinguished, painless, unboastful truth, in a crystalline household world of truth; gentle, through daily entreatings of gentleness, and honourable trusts, and pretty prides of child-fellowship in offices of good; strong, not in bitter and doubtful contest with temptation, but in peace of heart, and armour of habitual right, from which temptation falls like thawing hail; self-commanding, not in sick restraint of mean appetites and covetous thoughts, but in vital joy of unluxurious life, and contentment in narrow possession, wisely esteemed.—John Ruskin, in an introduction to Grimm's "German Popular Tales," *illustrated by Cruikshank.*

I. THE ROUSSEAU IMPETUS.

Mr. E. V. Lucas has compiled two volumes of old-fashioned tales for modern readers. In his introductions he analyses the qualities of his selected stories, and it is generally the case that, except for incidental detail, what is said of one of a kind might just as appropriately be meant for the other. If, at moments, the editor is prone to confuse quaintness with interest, he makes full amends by the quick humour with which he deals with the moral purpose. Perhaps it was part of the game for our great-grandfathers to expect didacticism, but simply because children were then considered "the immature young of men" is no excuse, although it may be a reason, for the artificiality which subserved play to contemplation. Wherever he can escape the bonds of primness, Mr. Lucas never fails to take advantage; the character of his selections indicates this as well as such critical remarks as the following:

"The way toward a nice appreciation of the child's own peculiar characteristics was, however, being sought by at least two writers of the eighteenth century, each of whom was before his time: Henry Brooke, who in 'The Fool of Quality' first drew a small boy with a sense of fun, and William Blake, who was the first to see how exquisitely worth study a child's mind may be."

Mr. Lucas brings together a number of stories by different persons, treating them as a group. Should you read them you will have a fairly distinct conception of early nineteenth century writing for children. But there is yet another way of approaching the subject, and that is by tracing influence from writer to writer, from group to group; by seeking for the *impetus* without which the story becomes even more of a husk than ever.

Let us conjure up the long row of theoretical children of a bygone age, painfully pathetic in their staidness, closely imprisoned. They began with

Jean Jacques Rousseau (1712–1778), the iconoclast, who attacked civil society, the family, the state, the church, and from whose pen the school did not escape chastisement. His universal cry of "back to nature" frightened the conservative; even Voltaire could not refrain, on reading the essay dealing with the origin of inequality among men, to write him: "Never has any one employed so much genius to make us into beasts. When one reads your book he is seized at once with a desire to go down on all-fours."

Rousseau's "Émile, or Treatise on Education" (1762) was wholly revolutionary; it tore down ancient theories, such as those practised by Dr. Isaac Watts upon his "ideal" boy and girl; all existent educational strictures were ignored. Rousseau applied to childhood his belief in the free unfolding of man's nature; however impracticable his methods, he loosed the chains that held fast the claims of childhood, and recognised their existence. He set the pendulum swinging in the human direction; he turned men's minds upon the study of the child as a child, and, because of this, takes his place at the head of modern education. He opened the way for a self-conscious striving on the part of authors to meet the demands of a child's nature, by furnishing the best literary diet—according to educational theories—for juvenile minds. Revolutionary in religious as well as in political and social ideals, Rousseau's educational machinery was destined to be infused, by some of his zealous followers, with a piousness which he never would have sanctioned.

Training should be natural, says Rousseau; the child should discover beauty, not be told about it; should recognise spontaneously what he is now taught. Education should be progressive; at the same time it should be negative. This sounds contradictory, but Rousseau would keep his child a child until the age of twelve; he would prevent him from knowing through any mental effort; he would have him grow like "Topsy" in animal spirits, his mind unbridled and imbibing facts as his lungs breathe in air. Yet inconsistency is evident from the outset: the child must observe, at the same time he must not remember. Is it possible, as Professor Payne challenges, to form the mind before furnishing it?

Rousseau's precepts are wise and brilliant. We hear him exclaiming: "It is less consequence to prevent him [the child] from dying than to teach him how to live;" "The man who has lived most is not he who has numbered the most years, but he who has had the keenest sense of life;" "The best bed is that which brings us the best sleep." These aphorisms are as apt as those of Franklin; but in their exercise it is necessary to consider the concomitants brought into play.

Émile is made an orphan; thus Rousseau gives himself full sway; thus does he free himself from the necessity of constant consultation with parents. He is determined to love the boy, to encourage him in his sports, to develop his amiable instincts, his natural self. Émile must not cry for the sweets of life; he must have a need for all things rather than a joyful desire for some. Instead of teaching virtue to him, Rousseau will try to shield him from a knowledge of all vice. Where Plato recommends certain pastimes, he will train Émile to delight in himself—thus making of him something of a youthful egoist. This amœba state, endowed with all physical liberty, deprived of all dignity of childish memory, is to be the boyhood of Émile. He "shall never learn anything by heart, not even fables and not even those of La Fontaine, artless and charming as they are." Though he does not possess the judgment to discriminate, he must be told the bare facts, and he must discover for himself the relations which these facts bear to each other. At the age of twelve, he shall hardly know a book when he sees it. Rousseau calls books "cheerless furniture."

So much for the boy; the girl Sophie fares as ill. Being of the woman kind as well as of the child brand, she is to develop in even a more colourless fashion. Fortunately all theory is not human actuality, and Émile must have peopled his world in a way Rousseau could not prevent. We are given natural rights and hereditary endowments; even the savage has his standards and his dreams. Rousseau's plan of existence ignored the social evolution of history. Yet Émile might by such training have been saved many wearisome explanations of the Mr. Barlow type, and it is ofttimes true, as Mr. G. K. Chesterton claims, that the mysteries of God are frequently more understandable than the solutions of man.

There was much in Rousseau's book to rouse opposition; there was equally as much to appeal to those whose instinctive love of childhood was simply awaiting the flood gates to be opened. Like the Grimm fairy tales of suspended animation, on the instant, the paternal instinct began to be active, the maternal instinct to be motherly. Rousseau—emended, modified, accentuated—overran England, France, and Germany. Children were now recognised as children; it remained to be seen whether they *were* to be children.

The didactic era is in no way more fitly introduced than with the names of Madame de Genlis and Arnaud Berquin in France, together with the Edgeworth and Aikin families and Thomas Day in England. To each, small space may be allotted, but they are worthy of full and separate consideration.

Stéphanie Félicité [Ducrest de St. Aubin], Comtesse de Genlis (1746–1830), is represented upon the library shelves by nearly a hundred volumes. They were written during the course of a varied existence, at the court of Louis XV and at home. Her *Mémoires* are told in a facile and delightful style, and indicate how she so thoroughly balanced the many conflicting elements in her duties that she remains for those days a rare example of wife, mother, society woman, and student. Her discernment of people, as revealed in these pages, was penetrating and on the whole just; and, though a typical product of her time, her nature was chastened by a refined and noble spirit.

The first glimpse she affords of herself is as a child of six, when she was taken to Paris. There, her brother was placed at a seat of learning, where the master guaranteed within six weeks' time to teach him reading and spelling by means of a system of counters. The little girl's teeth were shedding—not a prepossessing phase of growth at best. But, in addition, she was encased in whalebone stays, her feet were squeezed into tight shoes, her curls done up in corkscrew papers, and she was forced to wear goggles. The height of cruelty now followed. Country-bred as she had been, her manner was not in accord with the best ideas; her awkwardness was a matter of some concern. In order to give better poise to her head, a thick iron collar was clapped upon her supple throat. Here she was then, ready for regular lessons in walking. To run was to court disfavour, for little girls, especially city ones, were not allowed to do such an improper thing; to leap was an unspeakable crime; and to ask questions was an unwarranted license. It is small wonder that later on she should utilise the memory of such abject slavery in "The Dove," one of the numerous plays included in her "Theatre of Education."

Her early years thus prepared Madame de Genlis for the willing acceptance of any new educational system, especially one which would advocate a constant companionship between parents and child. For she had been reared with but exceptional glimpses of her father and mother; during one of these times she relates how the former, in his desire to make her brave, forced her to catch spiders in her hands. Such a picture is worthy a place by the side of Little Miss Muffet.

Like all children, Madame de Genlis was superior to her limited pleasures; she possessed an imagination which expanded and placed her in a heroic world of her own making. There is peculiar pleasure in discovering under narrow circumstances the good, healthy spirit of youth. Madame de Genlis seemed proud to record a certain dare-devil rebellion in herself during this period. The pendulum that is made to swing to its unnatural bent brings with the downward stroke unexpected consequences. And so, when she married De Genlis, it is no surprise to read that she did so secretly—a union which is most charmingly traced in the Memoirs.

She developed into a woman with deep religious sensibility; with forceful personality; with artistic talent, well exemplified by a masterly execution on the harp. Living in an atmosphere of court fêtes, the drama occupied no small part in her daily life. Whether at her Château Genlis or elsewhere, she was ever ready for her rôle in theatricals, as dramatist or as actress. She played in

Molière, and was accounted excellent in her characters; naught pleased her better than a disguise; beneath it her vivacity always disported itself.

Her interest in teaching began early; no sooner was she a mother than she hastened to fix her opinions as to the duties that lay before her, in a written treatise called "Reflections of a Mother Twenty Years of Age," views which in their first form were lost, but which were rehabilitated in the later "Adèle et Théodore," consisting of a series of letters on education.

After her mind had been drawn to the style of Buffon—for Madame de Genlis was a widely read woman—she determined upon improving her own manner of literary expression. She burned her bridges behind her, and fed the flames with all of her early manuscripts. Then she started over again to reconstruct her views, and in her study she made careful notes of what she fancied of importance for her future use. She was on intimate terms with Rousseau, took him to the theatre, and conversed with him on education chiefly, and about diverse matters generally. If she did not agree with him, Madame de Genlis was told that she had not as yet reached the years of discretion when she would find his writings suited to her. But Rousseau enjoyed the vivacious lady, who was kind-hearted and worth while talking to, notwithstanding the fact that she had the courtier's love of banter. She writes:

"Not to appear better than I am, I must admit that I have often been given to ridicule others, but I have never ridiculed anything but arrogance, folly, and pedantry."

Madame de Genlis was not a hero-worshipper; on first meeting Rousseau, his coat, his maroon-coloured stockings, his round wig suggested comedy to her, rather than gravity. We wonder whether she asked his advice regarding the use of pictures in teaching history, a theory which she originated and which Mrs. Trimmer was to follow in her Bible lessons. Full as the days were, Madame de Genlis, nevertheless, seems to have been able to give to her children every care and attention. This must have won the unstinted commendation of Rousseau, who preached that a boy's tutor should be his father, and not a hired person.

Madame de Genlis created her own theatre; she wrote little comedies of all kinds, which met with great success. Often these would be presented in the open air, upon platforms erected beneath the shade of forest trees; by means of the drama she sought to teach her daughters elementary lessons of life; the stage to her was an educational force. Through the plays her popularity and reputation increased to such an extent, that the Electress of Saxony demanded her friendship. She became instructress to the children of the Duke and Duchess of Chartres, and she prided herself upon being the first in France to adopt the foreign method of teaching language by conversation.[31] The rooms for her royal pupils were fitted according to her special indications. Rough sketches were made upon a wall of blue, representing medals, busts of kings and emperors of Rome. Dates and names were frescoed within easy view. Every object was utilised, even to the fire screens, which were made to represent the kings of France; and over the balustrades were flung maps, like banners upon the outer walls.

Up and down such staircases, and through such rooms wandered the cultivated flowers of royalty. They did not suffer, because their teacher was luckily human as well as theoretical; because she had a vein of humour as well as a large seriousness. Her whole educational scheme is described in her "Lessons of a Governess" and "Adèle et Théodore." When she engaged a tutor to attend to the special studies of the young prince in her charge, she suggested the keeping of an hourly journal which would record the little fellow's doings—each night she, herself, to write critical comments upon the margins of every page. In addition, she kept a faithful record of everything coming within her own observation; and this she read aloud each day to her pupils, who had to sign their names to the entries. But much to the chagrin of Madame de Genlis, the Duke and Duchess refused to take the time to read the voluminous manuscripts; they trusted to the wisdom and discretion of the teacher.

Not a moment was lost during these busy periods; history was played in the garden, and civic processions were given with ponies gaily caparisoned. Even a real theatre was built for them. Royalty was taught to weave, and was taken on instructive walks and on visits to instructive places. But, through all this artificiality, the woman in Madame de Genlis saved the teacher.

The latter part of her eventful life was filled with vexations, for the thunders of the French Revolution rolled about her. A short while before the storm broke, she went on a visit to England, where she came in contact with Fox and Sheridan, with Walpole and Reynolds; and where she paid a special visit to the House of Commons and was a guest at Windsor.

All told, here was a writer for children, self-conscious and yet ofttimes spontaneous in her style. She is interesting because of herself, and in spite of many of her literary attempts. She is little read to-day, in fact rarely mentioned among juvenile book lists; education killed a keen perception and vivacity by forcing them along prescribed lines. One glimpse of Madame de Genlis in old age is recorded by Maria Edgeworth, who called on her in 1803.

"She came forward, and we made our way towards her as well as we could, through a confusion of tables, chairs, and work-baskets, china, writing-desks and inkstands, and bird-cages and a harp.... She looked like the full-length picture of my great-great-grandmother Edgeworth you may have seen in the garret, very thin and melancholy, but her face not so handsome as my great-grandmother's; dark eyes, long sallow cheeks, compressed, thin lips, two or three black ringlets on a high forehead, a cap that Mrs. Grier might wear,—altogether an appearance of fallen fortunes, worn-out health, and excessive but guarded irritability. To me there was nothing of that engaging, captivating manner which I had been taught to expect by many even of her enemies; she seemed to me to be alive only to literary quarrels and jealousies; the muscles of her face as she spoke, or as my father spoke to her, quickly and too easily expressed hatred and anger whenever any not of her own party were mentioned."

A frontispiece to the 1802 edition of Arnaud Berquin's (1749–1791) works represents his bust being garlanded and crowned, and his "L'Ami des Enfans" being regarded by a group of admirers, both young and old. But though this very volume was received with honours by the French Academy, and though by it Berquin claims his right to immortality, French children of the present refrain from reading him as systematically as we refrain from reading "Sandford and Merton," which, as it happens, Berquin translated into French. There are popular editions of "L'Ami des Enfans," but children do not relish the tameness of such moral literature. The editor detailed to write Berquin's short life, which was spent in the study of letters, and in following up one "Ami" by another, sacrifices incident and fact for encomium. It is easy to claim for Berquin modesty and goodness during his residence in his native town near Bordeaux and after his arrival in Paris during 1772; it is interesting to know that he was encouraged to use his talents by the praise of his friends, but far more valuable would it have been to tell just in what manner he reached that ethical state which overflowed in his "L'Ami des Enfans," published during the years 1782 and 1783. The full purport of the volume is summed up exuberantly in the following paragraph:

"Quelle aimable simplicité! quel naturel! quel sentiment naïf respirent dans cette ingénieuse production! Au lieu de ces fictions extravagantes, et de ce merveilleux bizarre dans lesquels on a si longtemps égaré l'imagination des enfans, Berquin ne leur présente que des aventures dont ils peuvent être témoins chaque jour dans leur famille."

The tales and playlets written by Berquin are almost immoral in their morality. It is a question whether the interest of children will become absorbed by the constant iteration of virtue; whether goodness is best developed through the exploitation of deceit, of lying, of disobedience, and of wilful perverseness. To be kind means to be rewarded, to be bad is synonymous with punishment. Berquin and his followers might have drawn up a moral code book in pocket form, so stereotyped was their habit of exacting an eye for an eye and a tooth for a tooth. What are the punishments of vanity, what the outcome of playing when the afternoon task is to watch the sheep? The pictures made to illustrate the stories depict boys and girls kneeling in supplication, while the grown persons almost invariably stand in disdainful attitude. The children who would be their own masters and go out in a boat, despite parental warning, are upset: there is the algebraic formula. "Plainness the Dress of Use" is probably a worthy subject for a tale, and "A Good Heart Compensates for Many Indiscretions" a pathetic title for a play. But young people as a general rule are not maudlin in their feelings; even granting that there are some given that way, they should not be encouraged in holding a flabby standard of human, as well as of divine, justice. "L'Ami des Enfans" is filled with such sentimental mawkishness.

II. THE EDGEWORTHS; THOMAS DAY; MRS. BARBAULD; AND DR. AIKIN.

At the early age of twenty-three, Richard Lovell Edgeworth (1744–1817) decided to educate his son, Richard, according to the principles set down by Rousseau. He thrust the little fellow back into a state of nature by taking his shoes and stockings off and by cutting the arms from all his jackets. But, try as he did in every way to make a living Émile out of young Richard, the father found that the theories did not work. When he took the luckless boy to Paris and called upon Rousseau, there ensued an examination of results, and the sum-total was pronounced a failure. Hon. Emily Lawless writes in some glee:

"It is impossible to read without a smile of the eminently unphilosophic wrath expressed by the sage, because each time that a handsome horse or vehicle passed them on their walk, his temporary charge—a child of seven—invariably cried out, 'That's an English horse!' ... a view which he solemnly pronounced to be due to a sadly early 'propensity to party prejudice'!..."

Edgeworth lost entire faith in the practical application of the Rousseau scheme in after years; but the lasting effect it seems to have produced upon the unfortunate victim was to place him in the ranks of mediocrity, for he was hardly ever spoken of thereafter by his family; and in order to remove himself from further disturbance, as soon as he reached years of discretion, he hastened to place miles between himself and the scenes of his youth; Richard came to America.

Edgeworth's love affairs—for four times he was married—are involved, and do not concern us, save as they effect Thomas Day. But, personally, he enters our plan as influencing his daughter, Maria Edgeworth (1767–1849), with whom he wrote "Practical Education." There are some men—and Edgeworth was bordering on the type—who assume an almost dreadful position in a household; who torture the mind of boy or girl by prying, and by wishing to emphasise hidden meaning in everything; who make children fear to ask questions lest a lecture, dry and unoriginal, be the penalty. Such men have a way of fixing youth with intense, severe gaze—of smiling with a fiendish self-complacency over their own superiority—of raising their eyebrows and reprimanding should the child be watching the flight of a sparrow instead of being ever alert for an unexpected question or bit of information which a grown person might put to him on earth. Such men are the kind who make presents of Cobbet's "Advice to Young Men," and who write mistaken sentiments of nobility on the fly-leaf of Samuel Smiles's "Self-Help."

Edgeworth's redeeming trait was his earnest desire to bring the best within reach of his children, and he considered his severity the proper kind of guidance for them. Whatever sin of commission is to be laid to his charge, it is nevertheless true that it was not so great as to destroy the love Maria had for him. The literary critic has to reckon with the total amount of effect his teaching, his personal views had upon the writings of his daughter. That he did influence her is certain, and nowhere more thoroughly shown than in her work for children. In theory this work traces its origin to Rousseau, while in its modelling it bears a close relationship to Madame de Genlis and to Berquin.

Banish dolls is the cry in "Practical Education," and if you have toys in the nursery at all, let them be of a useful character—not mechanical novelties, but cubes, cylinders, and the like. Place before children only those pictures which deal with familiar objects, and see to it that the pose of every figure, where there are figures, is natural; a boy once went with Sir Joshua Reynolds through an art gallery, and invariably he turned with displeasure away from any form represented in a constrained attitude. This is the general tone of the Edgeworths as teachers.

The set notions that fill the pages of "Practical Education" often border on the verge of bathos. They leave no room for the exercise of spontaneous inclination; by their limitations, they recognise no great amount of common sense in others. They create in one a desire at times to laugh, and again a desire to shake the authors who were in the frame of mind to hold such views. There are certain instincts which are active by reason of their own natures,—and one is the love of parent for offspring. We even accredit the wild animal with this quality. When the Edgeworths declare that "My dear, have you nothing to do?" should be spoken in sorrow, rather than in anger, the advice irritates; it is platitudinous; it must have irritated many naturally good mothers, even in those days when such a tone in writers was more the rule than the exception.

On the subject of books Miss Edgeworth and her father become more interesting, though none the less startling in their suggestions. One of Maria's early tasks in 1782 had been to translate "Adèle et Théodore"; to her this book was worthy of every consideration. In the choice of reading for young folks, the two do not reach very much beyond their own contemporaries:

Mrs. Barbauld's "Lessons," the Aikin's "Evenings at Home," Berquin's "L'Ami des Enfans," Day's "Sandford and Merton" were recommended. And in addition there were mentioned Madame de Silleri's stories, known as the "Theatre of Education," Madame de la Fite's "Tales" and "Conversations," and Mrs. Smith's "Rural Walks." Despite the fact that fairy tales are at this period frowned upon as useless frivolities, "Robinson Crusoe," "Gulliver's Travels," "The Three Russian Sailors," and the "Arabian Nights' Entertainment" are suggested because of the interest and profit to be had in voyages and travels of all kinds. Fancy was thus held at a discount.

Two books of nature are mentioned, and curiously one is emphasised as of special value for children provided it is beforehand judiciously cut or blotted out here and there. The Edgeworths obtained this idea from an over-careful mother who was in the habit of acting as censor and editor of all juvenile books that found their way into her house. In Russia, the authorities take an ink pad and stamp out the condemned passages of any book officially examined. In the same summary manner, English parents were advised to treat their children's stories. The Edgeworths went even further, suggesting that, besides striking out separate words with a pen, it would be well to cut the undesirable paragraphs from the page, provided by so doing the sense of the text on the reverse side was not materially interfered with. To mark the best thoughts for young readers was also strongly recommended.

The authors are never wanting in advice. If children are good, what need is there to introduce them to evil in their stories? Evil is here meant in its mildest sense. They should be kept from all contagion. But bad boys and girls should be told to read, in "The Children's Friend," tales like "The Little Gamblers" and "Honesty is the Best Policy," which will teach them, by examples of wickedness, to correct their ways. Such strange classification suggests that literature was to be used as a species of moral reformatory. Two significant facts are to be noted in this chapter on books: there is an attempt to grade the literature by some age standard, bringing to light a gap between four and seven years which may be offset by a similar gap to-day; so, too, does there seem to have been, then as now, a great lack of history and biography.

The idea upon which the "Parent's Assistant" was founded began to shape itself in Miss Edgeworth's mind early in life. Left alone for a short period with her younger brothers and sisters, she manufactured tales for their edification, many of which, in after years, she utilised. In 1796 she gathered together and published some of her best stories, among them "The Purple Jar" and "Lazy Laurence." "Simple Susan" would probably not be so widely emphasised were it not for the fact that Sir Walter Scott recorded "that when the boy brings back the lamb to the little girl, there is nothing for it but to put down the book and cry."

Miss Edgeworth and her father had much preferred that the book be called "The Parent's Friend," for lodged in the former's memory were disagreeable thoughts of an old-time arithmetic which had plagued her early years, and was named "The Tutor's Assistant."

The theatricals performed in the Edgeworth household afforded much pleasure. It is very likely that the custom was gleaned from Madame de Genlis. Plays were written for every festive season. The publication of the "Parent's Assistant" suggested the acting of some of the playlets contained in the book. There seem to have been two theatres, one fitted up just over Richard Lovell's study, and another temporary stage erected in the dining-room. Here, one evening, was enacted the exemplary dialogue of "Old Poz," where a poor man is suspected, by a Justice, of stealing what a magpie has in reality secreted. Lucy, the good little daughter, clears the innocent fellow, upon whom her father sits in very stern, very unreasonable, and most unnatural judgment. Irritable to a degree, the Justice, who is positive about everything, shuts up any one who gainsays a word contrary to his obstinacy, but "Oh, darling," he remarks to his daughter, after her excellent deed, "*you* shall contradict me as often as you please." This method is neither more nor less than poisonous; it is polluted with a certain license which no good action ever sanctions. There is small doubt that children see the absurdity of it, for it cheapens right-doing in their eyes.

The compensating balance of good and bad is exercised to a monotonous degree in Miss Edgeworth's tales. There are the meek, innocent girl, and the proud, overbearing girl in "The Bracelet"; the heedless, extravagant boy, and the thoughtful, thrifty boy in "Waste Not, Want Not." Disaster follows disaster; reward courts reward. Not content with using these extremes of human nature in one story, Miss Edgeworth rings the changes, slightly altered in form, in others of her tales.

"The Purple Jar" in substance is the same as "Waste Not, Want Not"; the moral applications are identical. One has but to glance through the pages of the latter story to note its didactic pattern. Yet Miss Edgeworth possessed her literary excellencies in human characterisation, in that power of narrative which gained effect, not through ornamentation, but through deep knowledge of the real qualities of common existence. The dominant fault is that she allowed her ultimate object to become crystallised into an overshadowing bulwark, a danger which always besets the "moral" writer, and produces the ethical teacher in a most obtruding form. When Miss Edgeworth's little girl sprains her ankle and her father picks her up, she consciously covers her leg with her gown. Fate seems never to have worked so swiftly, so determinedly, as in those tales where thoughtless boys on their walks had the consequences of their bad acts visited upon them during the homeward journey. The hungry, the lame, the halt, the blind turn unexpected corners, either to wince beneath the jeers of one type of mortal child, or to smile thanks to the other kind for a gentle word or a much-needed penny.

No one can wholly condemn the tale, typified by Miss Edgeworth's "Parent's Assistant." Childhood is painted in quaint, old-fashioned colours, even though the staid little heroes and heroines have no interests. They take information into their minds as they would take physic into their bodies. They are all normal types, subjected to abnormal and unnaturally successive temptations, and given very exacting consciences. A writer in *Blackwood's* becomes indignant over such literary treatment:

"They [the girls] have good reason to expect from these pictures of life, that if they are very good and very pious, and very busy in doing grown-up work, when they reach the mature age of sixteen or so, some young gentleman, who has been in love with them all along, will declare himself at the very nick of time; and they may then look to find themselves, all the struggles of life over, reposing a weary head on his stalwart shoulder.... Mothers, never in great favour with novelists, are sinking deeper and deeper in their black books,—there is a positive jealousy of their influence; while the father in the religious tale, as opposed to the moral and sentimental, is commonly either a scamp or nowhere. The heroine has, so to say, to do her work single-handed."

What is true of these young people is therefore likewise true of their grown-up associates. They have definite personalities, and they are either monstrosities of excellence or demons of vice and temper. But here also a careful distinction was preserved. Mr. Lucas says in his "Old-Fashioned Tales":

"The parents who can do no wrong are very numerous; but they are, it should be pointed out, usually the parents of the central child. There are very often parents and relations of other and subsidiary children whose undesirable habits are exceedingly valuable by way of contrast."

Despite the fact that there is so much to condemn in this *genre* of writing, Miss Edgeworth was endowed with that sober sense and inexhaustible power of invention claimed for her by critics of the period. Her care for detail, her exhibition of small actions that mark the manners of all people in different walks of life, were distinguishing features of her skill.

With her father Miss Edgeworth laboured on other things besides the "Practical Education"; while the two were preparing the essay on "Irish Bulls," published in 1802, she plainly states that the first design was due to him, and that in her own share she was sedulously following the ideas suggested by him. Throughout her autobiographical data she offers us many glimpses of that family unity which existed—whether from voluntary desire or because of the domineering grip of Edgeworth, is not stated. She was continuously solicitous for his welfare, not through any forced sense of duty, but because of her desire to give pleasure in small ways; she found it agreeable to sit of an evening doing needle work, while Edgeworth "read out" Pope's Homer. In the course of such hours she first became acquainted with Scott's "Lady of the Lake" and "Waverley."

The friendship between Miss Edgeworth and Scott was deep and cordial; one was not without abiding influence on the other. She describes with graphic pen the first sound of his voice at Abbotsford; and the biographer has no more agreeable material to work upon than her fortnight spent as a guest of the novelist, and his return visit to Edgeworthtown in 1825.

For a man whose avowed detestation of women was well known to every one, Thomas Day (1748–1789) succeeded in leading a life of romantic variety. Yet he was not a person of strong passion; in fact, was more inclined to brooding melancholy. His intimacy with the Edgeworth family began when he met Richard Lovell at Oxford; and it was when he saw the training of Émile applied to his friend's son that his mind was seized with the idea of carrying out a similar scheme himself. He held a great contempt for dress; and his numerous vagaries regarding the conduct and duties of a wife were so pronounced that it is most likely they came between himself and Maria Edgeworth, with whom it is thought there was some romantic understanding.

Unlike Edgeworth, Day had no child to experiment upon. So he set about "breeding up" two girls, away from conflicting influences, and according to nature. One was obtained from an orphan asylum, and was known as Sabrina Sidney; the other, called Lucretia, was taken from a Foundling Hospital. In order to give a moral tone to the situation, these girls were bound out to Edgeworth, who was a married man. Not many knew that Day had hastened with both of the damsels to Avignon. Here he began to educate them with the intention of training one for his future wife.

Events did not progress smoothly, however; the girls quarrelled as saints would have quarrelled under the circumstances, and they occupied their time by falling out of boats and having smallpox. What their schooling consisted of may be imagined from the fragment of a letter written by Sabrina to Mr. Edgeworth:

"I hope I shall have more sense against I come to England—I know how to make a circle and an equilateral triangle—I know the cause of day and night, winter and summer."

At the advanced age of twenty-two—even younger than Edgeworth when he first became imbued with the Rousseau doctrines—Day returned to Lichfield—the home of Johnson and of Dr. Charles Darwin—bringing with him his charges: Lucretia, who was hopelessly dull, and Sabrina, who proved the favourite and was by far the more attractive of the two, with her fetching auburn ringlets, her long amorous eyelashes, and her very melodious voice. The young ladies had failed to become thoroughly steeled against the slings and arrows of outrageous fortune. In most respects they persisted in remaining like the average woman with sensibility. When hot sealing-wax was dropped upon the shapely arm of Sabrina, to harden her against the fear of pain, she refused to behave heroically; when a pistol was fired at her petticoats—a volley of lead for all she knew—her screams and frantic jumps indicated that her nerves were not impervious to the unexpected.

Day did not fail to show his disgust and disappointment. While Sabrina was at boarding-school, he hastened to forget all about her, and fell in love with Honora Sneyd, whose fame chiefly rests upon the fact that she was once courted by Major André. To make the situation more awkward, Edgeworth, despite his married state, likewise possessed strong affection for the same lady. She refused Day, and what followed contains the zest of a wicked little comedy. He fell ill, and had to be bled; then he summoned up sufficient strength to escape to France with Edgeworth, who felt it best to remove himself from temptation. It was during this trip that he visited Rousseau with poor little Richard. But before crossing the Channel, Day had succeeded in transferring his affections to Honora's sister, Elizabeth.

"Go," she said to him in substance, "try to assume some of the graces that you sorely lack. Learn to dress stylishly, and be taught the proper curl for a wig. Train yourself into a fashionable-looking husband, and come back to me."

Thus commanded, Day spent many weary hours wielding the foil, and being carried through the intricacies of the dance. And those legs of his—how he put them into exercise, hoping against hope to straighten them ere he returned to England!

But there was evidently no improvement in the end, for when the lady saw him, she unhesitatingly refused him. It is sufficient to say that, in time, Edgeworth married both sisters, Death regarding kindly his love of novelty.

With affections thus left high and dry, Day turned once more to Sabrina. He had long ago discarded Lucretia, who apprenticed herself to a milliner, and later became the wife of an honest draper. But Sabrina was fair to look upon and Day saw no reason why she should not satisfy his ideas of wifehood, provided she would dress according to his tastes. We applaud the shake of those auburn ringlets as she refused his wishes, and thus escaped matrimony with him.[32] There was another lady upon whom this honour was to descend.

When Miss Milnes, of Wakefield, was approached by Day, she was informed of all his requirements, and was deceived as to none of his vagaries. It must have been somewhat of a surprise to him when she accepted him, outlandish attire and all; and it is a pleasant disappointment to know that the marriage was a happy one, despite the fact that Mrs. Day insisted upon holding opinions of her own.

Day was most content when he was theorising; at the same time, it must not be lost sight of that he had timely interests. His feelings were strongly aroused against the state of negro slavery in America, and he was earnest in his advocacy of parliamentary reform. His great fault was that he was always carried to extremes whenever good motives prompted him. His earnest concern for the poor, during 1781, was accompanied by stern denials of pleasures for himself,—well-nigh of the necessities of life.

Day realised the failures of his theories as applied to grown people; had he not done so, we most likely would not have had "Sandford and Merton." His attention was soon attracted to the infant mind as an unworked field; the Edgeworths were meeting success with their children's books; he would attempt the same thing, and so, during 1783, 1787, and 1789, the three successive volumes of his famous story appeared—an elongated "Waste Not, Want Not."

Day had heretofore suggested a certain effeminate bearing in his character; he recognised it, and was now suddenly beset with a consuming desire to supplant this manner by an overtowering manliness, by the exercise of firmness and strength. But the new policy was to prove his undoing. On the afternoon of September 28, 1789, he went to ride on an unbroken horse, believing to curb him by the discipline of command rather than of the stock. The animal took fright and threw him; he received injuries from which he almost immediately died. On the evidence of Miss Seward, it is recorded that Mrs. Day thereafter "lay in bed, into the curtains of which no light was admitted, ... and only rose to stray alone through her garden when night gave her sorrows congenial gloom."

The estimate of such a work as "Sandford and Merton" cannot be based upon modern standards; all of the factors characteristic of the didactic writers for children, such as persistent questioning, the encyclopædic grown person in the shape of Mr. Barlow, and the monotonous interchange of narrative and dialogue, are employed as vehicles for knowledge. The book is unique, inasmuch as it sought to supply a variety of stories suitable in style and content for the beginner.

"The only method I could invent," writes Day, "was to select such passages of different books as were most adapted to their experience and understanding. The least exceptionable that I could find for this purpose were Plutarch's Lives, and Zenophon's History of the Institution of Cyrus, in English translations; with some part of Robinson Crusoe, and a few passages in the first volume of Mr. Brook's Fool of Quality."

In those days, if authors are to be believed, birds were in the habit of alighting on the hands of good children; they are more timid now, though children are not less good. The poor boy was made to feel how kind the good rich boy was to him throughout his shocking adversity; we are more considerate today. And so, Tommy Merton and Harry Sandford, products of a stilted age, are clad in uniforms similar to those worn by Miss Edgeworth's children. They are endowed with no exceptional qualities, with no defined will power; they stand in a long row of similarly subjected slaves of theory.

Miss Agnes Repplier calls this story one of her early moral pitfalls. She read it at a period when information was being forced down her, and "which," so she writes, "I received as responsively as does a Strassburg goose its daily share of provender."

Among the writers of this period, none are more important than Anna Letitia Aikin Barbauld (1743–1825). Her position is a unique one, for, being acquainted with all of her literary contemporaries and subject to their influence, she stands in a transition stage. Through her mental independence, she succeeded partially in breaking from the introspective method of motive-hunting, and foreshadowed the possibilities of Mrs. Hemans, the Brontés, and Mrs. Browning. She was reared in an atmosphere of intellectuality by her father, John Aikin, a professor and a man of advanced opinions regarding female instruction, two points which argued for her less conventional mind and for her less stilted manner.

When she married Rochemont Barbauld, who had been a student under her father, and who was a non-conformist, she was well versed in Greek and Latin, and in every way was equipped to do literary work. She was more or less influenced by her husband's religious independence; he changed his congregation from English Presbyterianism to Unitarianism, and it is not surprising to find the English public looking somewhat askance at Mrs. Barbauld's fitness to write for children. Madame de Genlis was in like fashion criticised for the religious views she held, and we shall find Miss More subject to the same scrutiny. The Aikins were the first to introduce the material lines in children's literature, "but the more anxiously religious mothers felt a certain distrust of the absence of direct lessons in Christian doctrines; and Mrs. Trimmer was incited to begin a course of writing for young people that might give the one thing in which, with all their far superior brilliancy, the Aikins were felt to be deficient."

We are not concerned with all of Mrs. Barbauld's work; she used to write poetry, some of it in repartee vein which struck the acute fancy of Charles Lamb; her essays were of an exceptional order, in a few instances expressed in imitation of Johnson; he himself had to acknowledge that of all who tried to ape him, she was most successful. Her educational opinions, sent from time to time in letters to Mrs. Montague, marked her ability as a teacher; but the method that she believed in was well nigh Socratic and ofttimes wearisome in its persistency; history and geography were given to infant minds in the form of lectures. Around 1802 William Godwin, of whom we shall have something to say later in his connection with the Lambs, wrote:

"I think Mrs. Barbauld's little books admirably adapted, upon the whole, to the capacity and amusement of young children.... As far as Mrs. Barbauld's books are concerned, I have no difficulty. But here my judgment and the ruling passion of my contemporaries divide. They aim at cultivating one faculty; I should aim at cultivating another.... Without imagination, there can be no genuine ardour in any pursuit or for any acquisition, and without imagination there can be no genuine morality, in profound feeling of other men's sorrow, no ardent and persevering anxiety for their interests. This is the faculty which makes the man, and not the miserable minuteness of detail about which the present age is so uneasy."

Childless herself, Charles Aikin was adopted by Mrs. Barbauld, the little Charles of "Early Lessons for Children," composed especially for him. The latter work was followed by "Hymns in Prose for Children," consisting of translations from all tongues, put into simple language, and not into verse, for fear they might fail to reach the comprehension otherwise. These hymns are probably most representative of Mrs. Barbauld's individual writings, for the work by which she is best known, the "Evenings at Home," was written in collaboration with her brother, Dr. Aikin.

In the "Evenings" a new tone is detected; despite a stilted style, the two authors aroused an interest in external objects, and, by their descriptions and suggestions, attempted to infuse meaning into the world surrounding the child. This small departure from the sectarian tendency prevailing in so much of the literature of that period, imperceptible though it may be, was due to a shifting of attitude toward women which was taking place in England. Mrs. Barbauld might be considered a "bold" example of feminine intellect reaching out for a larger sphere. We read that Fox was surprised that a woman could exhibit such clearness and consistency of viewpoint as were to be discovered in such of her essays as "Monastic Institutions"; and there were others who wondered at the alertness and interest she manifested in all matters pertaining to public affairs. Her force of intellect pleased some, her manner others. Scott confessed that her public reading of poetry inspired him to court the muse; Wordsworth unfolded so far as to envy the beauty of her stanzas on "Life," which toward the end contain these attractive, hopeful, and faith-abiding lines:

"Life! we've been long together,

Through pleasant and through cloudy weather;

'Tis hard to part when friends are dear;

Perhaps 'twill cost a sigh, a tear;

Then steal away, give little warning,

Choose thine own time;

Say not good-night, but in some brighter clime,

Bid me good-morning."

Mrs. Barbauld was one of a group of women writers, seeking through the force of their opinions to destroy the conventional barriers which kept the exercise of feminine minds within prescribed bounds. Harriet Martineau has outlined the tyrannical limitations which beset a young girl of the early nineteenth century; decorum stood for mental annihilation. When genteel persons came to call at the home of Jane Austen, the latter, out of regard for family feeling, and for fear of being thought forward and unmaidenly, was constrained to cover her manuscript with a muslin scarf.

Mrs. Barbauld did not make any revolutionary declaration, nor attempt any public defiance of custom; however, she did, by her reaching toward the manifest facts of life, secularise our concern for the common things about us. She encouraged, through her plea for the freedom of thought, the movement which resulted in the emancipation of her sex, and which found vent, on the one hand, in Mary Wollstonecraft's[33] "The Right of Woman" (1792) and, on the other, with more determined force, in John Stuart Mill's "On the Subjection of Women" (1869). As this freedom became more and more assured, there underwent a change in the educational attitude; a girl's mind had something more to work on than the motto of a sampler; her occupations became somewhat altered. And the women writers began to emphasise, in their stories for children, the individual inclinations of hero and heroine.

Wherever Charles Lamb discourses upon books, he assumes the critical attitude that deals with literature as a living force, as something built for human appeal. He met Mrs. Barbauld and Mrs. Trimmer on several occasions, and we can imagine the delight he took in shocking their ladylike senses by his witty and sudden remarks. At one period some dispute and ill-feeling existed between himself and Mrs. Barbauld, due to a false report that she had lampooned his drama, "John Woodvil."

Elia was not the sort of literary devotee to sanction anemic literature for children; his plea was for the vitalising of the nursery book. On October 23, 1802, he wrote to Coleridge:

"Mrs. Barbauld's stuff has banished all the old classics, ... and the shopman at Newbery's hardly deign'd to reach them off an exploded corner of a shelf, when Mary ask'd for them. Mrs. B's and Mrs. Trimmer's nonsense lay in piles about. Knowledge insignificant and vapid as Mrs. B's books convey, it seems, must come to a child in the shape of knowledge, and his empty noddle must be turned with conceit of his own powers, when he has learnt that a horse is an animal, and Billy is better than a horse, and such like; instead of that beautiful interest in wild tales which made the child a man while all the time he suspected himself to be no bigger than a child."

He saw the penalty that lay in cramming the child with natural history instead of furnishing him with some creative appeal. We can forgive Elia all his pranks when he thus pleads the genial claim of imagination; if, in a witty vein, he called Mrs. Barbauld and Mrs. Inchbald the "bald" old women, we must understand that Lamb had his petulant hours, and that children's literature of the day was sufficient to increase them!

The purport of "Evenings at Home" is instruction. Within the compass of a few pages, objects crowd one upon the other as thick and as fast as virtues do in Miss Edgeworth. Such keenness and alertness in observing common things, as are cultivated in "Eyes and No Eyes," stagger the intellect. It is well to teach your young companions to feel the hidden possibilities of nature and to cultivate within them a careful observation; but there is a vacation time for the mind, and the world, though it may be a school-room, is also a very healthy place to play in. Mr. Andrews, the immaculate teacher, is represented by the artist, in my copy of the book, as seated in a chair, with a compass in one hand resting upon a book, while behind him stretches the outline of a map; the two boys stand in front of him like prisoners before the bar. Here then is a new algebraic formula in the literature for the young.

Mrs. Barbauld thus represents a transition stage in juvenile writing; education and narrative walk side by side. She made it possible, in the future, for Peter Parley and for Rollo to thrive. Thomas Day foreshadowed the method of retelling incidents from the classics and from standard history and travel,— a form which is practised to a great extent by our present writers, who thread diverse materials on a slender wire of subsidiary story, and who, like Butterworth and Knox, invent untiring families of travellers who go to foreign parts, who see things, and then who talk out loud about them.

But before this secularisation gained marked hold, a new tributary is to be noted, which flowed into the moral stream,—a tributary which afforded the moral impulse a definite field to work in, which centred its purpose upon a distinct class. For heretofore the writers of juvenile literature had aimed for a general appeal. The struggle was now to be between the Sunday-school and the text-book.

III. The Sunday-school; Raikes; Hannah More; Mrs. Trimmer.

If the Sunday-school movement had not assumed some proportions about this time, it would have been necessary to create a practical outlet for the moral energy which dominated the authors of whom we have been writing. Had Robert Raikes not conceived his plan when he did, the ethical impulse would have run riot in a much wilder fashion, and would have done no good at all. For, whatever may be said against the old-time Sunday-school in a critical vein, one cannot ignore that its establishment brought immediate benefit. As it was, the new institution furnished the objective point for which the didactic school was blindly groping, and developed the idea of personal service. The social ideal was beginning to germinate.

Robert Raikes (1735 or 6–1811) was by profession a printer. He was of benevolent disposition and met with much to arouse his sympathy for the lower classes, whom he found indifferent to religion and hopelessly uncouth in their daily living. With the religious revival which swept through England around 1770, caused by the preaching of George Whitefield, Raikes began his work in earnest, first among the city prisons, where he was brought in contact with surprising conditions which had long lain in obscurity because of a wide-spread public indifference.

His observation thus trained to follow along this particular social line, he soon became attracted toward the children apprenticed to a certain pin factory. He saw that the discipline of work, however exacting, however it denied them the care and attention due to all young persons, was the only restrictive guidance they had. When Sunday came, they ran wild, relieved of duty, and not imbued with any idea of personal control. Their elders were living immoral lives; they had no opportunity or incentive to improve; and their natural inclination was to follow animal impulse and blind desire. To such a religious man as Raikes, the mandate, "Suffer little children to come unto me," was most naturally suggested by such circumstances. Some means of occupying these children on the Sabbath day must be devised.

So it was that on January 26, 1781, the first Sunday-school was opened. Raikes poured his whole energy into organization, and, through the medium of his own paper, the Gloucester *Journal*, spread broadcast his written suggestions about the work to be done, and his descriptions of the particular localities which most needed attention. He was in a position to gain publicity, and his own personal earnestness counted for a great deal. Already we have noted his relationship to Newbery, whose literary connections probably afforded Raikes some assistance.

The movement had been of five years' growth, when, in 1786, Raikes was summoned before King George III. Their Majesties, both the King and Queen, were interested by what they had heard, and wished to know something more. The Queen was being almost daily enthused through the intensity of Mrs. Trimmer's pleadings. This good lady, already known for her children's books, had put into operation a Sunday-school of her own at Brentwood, and it was to this that the King had paid a memorable visit, leaving behind him a reputation for "kind and condescending behaviour," which won the hearts of all the children. In this way was the official sanction placed upon Christianity as a practical force; there was even every prospect of starting a Sunday-school at Windsor. "A general joy reigns among the conductors," cried the enthusiastic Mrs. Trimmer, when she realised what interest was being shown in every quarter.

The programme framed for Raikes's little protégés was indeed sufficiently full to keep them from the highways. He writes:

"The children were to come after ten in the morning, and stay till twelve; they were then to go home and return at one; and after reading a lesson, they were to be conducted to Church. After Church, they were to be employed in repeating the catechism till after five, and then dismissed, with an injunction to go home without making a noise."

Lamb and Leigh Hunt, when together at Christ Hospital, were regarded as veritable monks in their knowledge of the Bible; but these little waifs were slaves of a rigorous order; there was nothing voluntary in their desire for spiritual light. The time was to arrive when more sunshine was to be mixed with the teaching, but in the beginning it was necessary for Raikes to keep the Sabbath forcibly observed rather than to devise a less exacting routine. He went about, untiring in his efforts; he plead personally with parents, besides hoping that, through the moral instruction being given to their children, they might be made to see the outlet for their own salvation.

Years after, testimony was obtained from the survivors of Raikes's discipline. One William Brick had been a scholar of his, and the memory of those days was vivid—perhaps a little too much so, but none the less picturesque:

"I can remember Mr. Raikes well enough," he said. "I remember his caning me. I don't suppose I minded it much. He used to cane boys on the back of a chair. Some terrible bad chaps went to school when I first went.... I know the parents of one or two of them used to walk them to school with 14-lb. weights tied to their legs, to keep them from running away.... When a boy was very bad, he would take him out of the school, and march him home and get his parents to 'wallop' him. *He'd stop and see it done*, and then bring the young urchin back, rubbing his eyes and other places.... Every one in the city loved and feared him."

Such a scene is not prepossessing; nor does moral suasion appear to have been as efficacious as the rod. Besides which, Raikes had a way of looking at a trembling victim through his reading-glass, and exclaiming in thunderous voice: "Ah, I can see you did not say your prayers this morning." An old man of eighty spoke of this circumstance with deep feeling; and, in awe-stricken tones, he ended by saying: "The boys believed he could see through stone walls with that glass; *and it magnified his eye*, so that they were sometimes frightened, and told wonderful stories about what Mr. Raikes could do with his wonderful glass."

The immediate influence this movement had upon children's books was to create a demand for tracts. Later on, after Thomas Carlyle, in 1839, had plead the cause of London public libraries, it suggested a special class of library as a part of the Sunday-school machinery. A general call was raised for juvenile books of a strictly religious nature, with an appeal intended for a poorer class of readers. Miss Hannah More represents the chief exponent of this grade of writing. "All service ranks alike with God," says Browning. But these ladies, who were untiring in their devotion to the cause, who were, in their parochial character, forerunners of the social worker of to-day, each was known through her special interest. We speak of Miss Catherine Sinclair, author of "Holiday House," as the first to introduce benches in the parks of Edinburgh, as the originator of drinking-fountains, as the founder of cooking-depots; of Priscilla Wakefield as the originator of savings-banks for the poor; of Miss More as the author of tracts; and of Mrs. Elizabeth Oakes Smith, one of the forgotten New-England writers, as the first to draw attention to the condition of the newsboys. Mrs. Trimmer, therefore, is justly connected with the history of the development of Sunday-schools.

In a tabular indication of the trend of juvenile literature, Sarah Kirby Trimmer (1741–1810) may be said to have been a disciple of Madame de Genlis and of Mrs. Barbauld, quite as much as a follower of Rousseau and of Raikes; she inherited from her father an overweening religious inclination, and several glimpses of her in the society of the day reveal how deeply seated her serious nature was. In London she talked with Dr. Johnson, Mr. Gainsborough, and Mr. Hogarth, and, through recognised powers of reading aloud, she charmed many of her friends. But it was a hopeless situation to cope with in a young girl, when, a dispute having arisen between Sir Joshua Reynolds and one of his friends, Sarah, being called upon to settle the point—a doubtful passage in "Paradise Lost"—drew the volume from the pocket of her skirt! At twenty-one she was married, destined to be the mother of six sons and six daughters, and no sooner was the first child born than she directed all of her attention, as Madame de Genlis did, to the subject of education.

Wearisome it is to come in contact with a person of one idea. Mrs. Trimmer naïvely confesses in her journal that she must have worn out the patience of many a visitor with her views upon education. As the years advanced, her opinions became more narrowed and more sectarian.

Mrs. Trimmer exhibited piety which was of the emotional, almost of the hysterical kind, yet sincere in its whole-souled acceptance of Bible truths. She questioned nothing; she believed with a simple faith that lacked proportion. One has to view her entirely from the standpoint of this single interest which had her under complete control. In her "Guardian of Education" she dwelt much upon the dangerous matter contained in children's books; in her "New Plan of Education" she condemned any attempt to extend the scope of education for the poor. Her chief motive in both cases was to keep away from faith any cause of its possible undoing. The earnestness put into her charity work, her untiring devotion to the Sunday-school, a certain gentle charm of conversation won for Mrs. Trimmer wide-spread attention. Her life was guided by the belief in a divine mission; her days were well ordered, from the hours before breakfast, which she reserved for the learning of poetry, to the evenings, when she would give herself up to meditation and prayer. In fact, during twenty-five years, she kept a diary, penned in secret moments of retreat, a curious display of over-welling feeling—pietistical neurasthenia. These pages are hardly to be considered interpretative—they are outpourings, giving one an awful sense of unworthiness, if life consists simply in submitting to biblical strictures and in uttering biblical paraphrases.

But Mrs. Trimmer was withal an active little woman, whose three hours, spent every Sunday over her journal, represented meditation only: in her practise of Christianity she was zealous; and her pen was employed in preparing the kind of food to foster a proper feeling among children and cottagers and *servants*. In this latter respect there was a change indeed from Miss Edgeworth, who considered the advisability of separating young people entirely from any possible contact with servants.

Among her children and her grandchildren, Mrs. Trimmer exerted profound influence; the Sabbath day was observed with great strictness; toys set aside while Stackhouse's "Commentary on the Bible"[34] was brought forth to look at; stories were told, and the progress of Bible heroes traced upon maps of the Holy Land. The spirit of rest and peace followed Mrs. Trimmer, who was averse to reading books of controversy. We are given a picture of her in her venerable old age, walking with her grandson among the plants and flowers, while she explained, with a certain lyric simplicity, the truths, as she saw them with her meek spirit, underlying the growth of the grass; and described the flight of a sparrow which escaped not the notice of God. There was thus unfolded to this little boy the holiness of all things in nature, permeated with a divine grace; he was made to consider the lilies of the field, and not a bush but might become to him a burning flame, not a stone but might be rent asunder by the resurrection of a dried-up seed.

Mrs. Trimmer's "Easy Lessons for Children," her "Easy Introduction to the Knowledge of Nature," her "Sacred History for Young Persons," and her works explaining the catechism, were among the rare books available for the purposes of Raikes's followers. They were easily understood; they explained satisfactorily for children, according to grown-up standards, certain religious teachings. In the Catholic church to-day, Mother Loyola is said to possess that same ability to unfold the meaning of the most difficult doctrine so that Catholic children can understand. Priests turn to her books rather than trust to their own interpretations. The general interest aroused for the poor, for the lower classes, appealed to Mrs. Trimmer; she became wholly absorbed; she wrote "The Servant's Friend" and edited a "Family Magazine," intended for their special instruction and amusement. Adopting Madame de Genlis's idea of using prints as a factor in nursery education, she prepared a series of illustrations from ancient history and from the Old Testament; and was further engaged in the simplification of Roman and English history for young readers.

The book that has come down to us as representing Mrs. Trimmer's work, "The History of the Robins," is a nature story of no mean value, easy in narrative and full of appeal for very young persons who are interested in simple incident. To American readers it is now available in a cut-up state, for Dr. Edward Everett Hale, in editing it, called the style "stilted" and diffuse, and thought that its unity could better be preserved by dealing only with the robins, and not at all with the extraneous doings of the Benson family.

When the Lambs removed to Enfield in 1827, Thomas Westwood, a boy of thirteen, lived near them. It was not long before he and Elia were on intimate terms, and he must have had exceptional merit for Lamb to give him free entrée to his books. "Lamb," so he has recorded, "initiated me into a school of literature which Mrs. Trimmer might not have considered the most salutary under the circumstances. Beaumont and Fletcher, Webster, Farquhar, Defoe, Fielding,—these were the pastures in which I delighted to graze in those early years; and which, in spite of Trimmer, I believe did me less evil than good."

An alteration in attitude appears to have been going on in several directions; the social strata were readjusting themselves. For Hannah More (1745–1833), it is claimed, stood at the parting of the roadways, where clergymen and schoolmasters, once frowned upon as quite inferior beings, now took positions of a higher nature. Had Miss More not thrown herself so heartily into the moral movement, she might have occupied a much more important position in English letters than she does. One cannot help feeling that, by the part she took in the Sunday-school development, she sacrificed her genius to a cause. In the biographies of these well-intentioned writers for children and for poor people, it is always satisfactory to linger, wherever opportunity presents, on the genial aspects of their lives; they are estimated in criticism so greatly by the weight, or by the lack of weight, of their ideas, that the human value which existed at the time is often lost sight of. However dry their preachments, their social lives were warmed by human intercourse and human service. It is hard to forget such a group as Scott, Maria and Patty Edgeworth, and others, listening to Patty while she sang Irish melodies. A similar scene is associated with Sally and Hannah More when they went to call on Dr. Johnson. He was not at home, and the two, left together in the autocrat's sanctum, disported themselves in mock humour. Hannah approached his great chair, and sat pompously in it, hoping to catch some of his genius. Can you not hear Johnson's laughter as he bluntly told her, when he was informed of the incident, that he rarely sat in that particular chair?

Mrs. Barbauld was no less clever than Hannah More in the handling of witty verse; in fact, the latter was ever ready with her gifts in the drawing-room, and added generously her share to the circle gathered around the actor, David Garrick. He it was who had sufficient faith in Miss More's dramatic ability to present two of her plays. Even at that time she had a reputation among her associates for being very strict in her religious observances; for one evening, it being Sunday, and Garrick not averse to piano-playing, he turned to "Nine," as he called her, thus indicating that she was a favoured one among the muses, and told her to leave the room, promising to call her back when the music was over.

Hannah More's social work is to be considered from the year (1789) that Mr. Wilberforce, one of her close friends, discovered the deplorable conditions existing in the districts around Cheddarcliff. Her long intercourse with the Garricks, and her various literary endeavours which took form during 1782 in her "Sacred Dramas" for the young, have no direct bearing upon her connection with the religious movement which places her in the general scheme with Robert Raikes and Mrs. Trimmer. Patty More had had, at an earlier period, large experience in school-teaching, and this was to prove of inestimable service, for it was with her assistance that Hannah carried on the work in the Mendip mining districts. The two met with some opposition, not only from the classes for whom they were specially striving, but from those who, less broad than themselves, held views regarding the Sunday-school that placed spirituality above the actual needs of the poverty-stricken communities. But, throughout, the Mores never swerved from their set purpose, even though illness overtook them and made the situation still harder than it was. For they were forced to ride many miles from their home, at first unknown in the region they had elected to benefit, a region cursed by ignorance, plagued by license, and wherein assault was a common incident.

"Miss Wilberforce would have been shocked," writes Hannah More, "could she have seen the petty tyrants whose insolence we stroked, the ugly children we fondled, the pointers and spaniels we caressed, the cider we commended, and the wine we swallowed."

A study of the centres established by these sisters, and which gradually exerted an influence over twenty-eight miles of territory, a distance traversed in a manner not unlike the journey of the circuit-riders who are to be met with throughout the mountain districts of the South, would throw considerable light on English labour conditions as they then existed. The setting is an isolated wild land, thus described by Miss More:

"Several of the grown-up youths had been tried at the last assizes; three were the children of a person lately condemned to be hanged; many thieves,—all ignorant, profane, and vicious beyond belief. Of this banditti, we have enlisted 170; and when the clergyman, a hard man, who is also the magistrate, saw these creatures kneeling around us, whom he had seldom seen but to commit, or punish in some way, he burst into tears."

The work grew with the months, and mention is soon made of nine hundred children flocking to a Mendip feast—little ones whose brightest moments were centred in the regular visits of these ministering ladies.

Miss More's powers were exerted toward counteracting the ideas being spread by the French Revolution; both high and low were struggling against them; they nearly swamped the genius of Wordsworth. Though she rejoiced in the fall of the Bastille, she deplored the deification of Nature and the reign of Reason, and vented her sarcasm on the philosophy of Paine. Her chief alarm was felt for the effect such opinions might have upon the middle class of England. But, despite her conservatism, Miss More was regarded as too strong-minded for religious work; the High Church accused her of too marked an independence. She was advised, much to her own amusement, to publish a confession of her faith. The discussion which ensued need not occupy us; it may, perhaps, have infused into her juvenile tracts a more determined tone, but it did not originally encourage her in their composition.

This was brought about through a desire to give the children of the poor districts religious literature as soon as they were able to read. Mrs. Trimmer was the only author then available, and her books were too expensive for the masses. The More sisters, therefore, soliciting the interest of the Duke of Gloucester, brother of George III, began the publication of the tracts, three a month, containing short talks, ballads, and moral tales. These were scattered broadcast over the country. The scheme lasted from 1794 to 1797, when they were forced to discontinue it, for lack of pecuniary backing. But, during the time, collections of "Repository Tracts" had been brought into existence, which, for at least a quarter of a century, were to stand representative of the best kind of reading for the poor.

A long list of books comprises the literary activity of Hannah More,[35] but it is by such volumes as her "Christian Morals," "Hints toward Forming the Character of a Young Princess [Charlotte, Princess of Wales]," "Practical Piety," "The Spirit of Prayer," "Strictures on the Modern System of Female Education," and "Thoughts on the Importance of Manners" that her genuine art is overclouded. In her "Repository Tracts," she was content to approach the poor as a class, nor was she willing to allow herself to forget for an instant that, because of their poverty, they were a type of inferior being. Her object was to make them content with their lot in life, and to have them feel comfortable and worthy within their particular sphere. They were potential with the strength that might place them at the head of their class, but could not carry them outside of it. An insurmountable barrier was thought to stretch between the high and low.

"The Shepherd of Salisbury Plain" is considered the most famous of Miss More's tracts. They all are redolent with the common moral ideal, but the local colour in them is real and the glimpses of the poor people, their homes, customs, beliefs, hopes, and despairs are described with minute vividness and with much feeling. Whatever brightness they contain is the sort that is gained by way of contrast,—an ethical resolve to show that things are not so bad that they may not still be worse. "Father," says the little girl, "I wish I was big enough to say grace. I am sure I would say it heartily to-day; for I was thinking what *poor* people do who have no salt to their potatoes."

The standard is a narrow one; the child who does not go to church is the bad child; the lack of a new gown fades before the delights over owning a new Bible. Instead of marking books, as the Edgeworths advised, Miss More italicised the passages worthy of memorising. Honest toil is the subject-matter of these stories; the village is the scene of many a vexation. The gaining of knowledge is only a means toward a better understanding of the catechism; one's duty is to learn to read, else the Holy Writ is a closed subject. There is no aim to carry the children outside of themselves by means of the highest imagination; they are told how they are to cope with their own environment, how to remain satisfied with their own station. They must be rich Christians, but still remain poor people.

Although Walpole retracted some of the harsh censure which he at first heaped upon Hannah More, he was not far wrong in his condemnation of her "ill-natured strictures." The person who does not recognise a tendency, in all this literature, "to protract the imbecility of childhood," "to arrest the understanding instead of advancing it," "to give forwardness without strength" has failed to understand the true function of a child's book—to afford the nursery a good time, is the way Mr. Lucas expresses it.

Was there not something in this religious one-sidedness to belittle the true dignity of the spirit?[36] Heaven lies about us in our infancy, and we find ourselves in a beautiful land of promise; we are placed therein to face the years; by experience, by training, by guidance along the lines of our own natures, we are prepared to understand something of the character of the way we shall have to tread alone. We should be made to face the future, but not to discount the present. We find ourselves defined by circumstances, but we need not remain slaves to them. To stigmatise a class in literature is to stigmatise a reader. Miss More and her contemporaries never questioned their social attitude—whether it was just or broad or transitory. Full of the pioneer work which they were doing, they did not recognise the right for the poor which was already the right for the rich. Juvenile literature was not for the heart of all youth, but for the benefaction of this one and of that. And while the educational idea broadened and was to advance with the scientific spirit on the one hand, on the other, it had narrowed and was destined for a long, monotonous struggle with the conscious Sunday-school tale. This character of story was flat and void, and, because removed from the reality of nature, it was robbed of the inherent spirit of truth. It identified religion with literary meekness.

IV. THE POETS: WATTS; JANE AND ANN TAYLOR; WILLIAM BLAKE.

Everything depends on the reality of a poet's classic character. If he is a dubious classic, let us sift him; if he is a false classic, let us explode him. But if he is a real classic, if his work belongs to the class of the very best (for this is the true and right meaning of the word classic, classical), then the great thing for us is to feel and enjoy his work as deeply as ever we can, and to appreciate the wide difference between it and all work which has not the same high character. This is what is salutary, this is what is formative; this is the great benefit to be got from the study of poetry. Everything which interferes with it, which hinders it, is injurious.—Matthew Arnold, in "The Study of Poetry."

We have progressed sufficiently in our outline to begin showing the links that bind the past with the present. To dwell upon more writers of the generation just treated is simply to repeat the same essential characteristics of the type. These authors all used the medium of prose in their desire to give young people books suitable to their comprehension. But there were a few poets who braved the intricacies of verse, and who wrote some very simple and pleasing lyrics, which have survived the change in spirit, and form some of the most agreeable pages in our children's anthologies. It will be recollected that Mrs. Barbauld feared poetry would not be understood, and so she wrote her volume of prose pieces which acted as a substitute.

Wordsworth himself could not have demanded a more careful attention to the simplicity of word selection than that paid by Dr. Isaac Watts (1674–1748), who, though not first in the field of hymn-writers, for his immediate predecessor was Bishop Thomas Ken[37] (1637–1711), author of "Morning and Daily Hymns," was nevertheless one of the very first consciously to pen a book of verse for a juvenile public.

Not only was he actively engaged in the interests of education, but, during his famous thirty-six years' spent as visitor in the household of Sir Thomas Abney, of Newington, he crystallised his ideas on education, and incorporated them in his "The Improvement of the Mind: To which is added A Discourse on the Education of Children and Youth."

This treatise may be regarded as a fair example of the pre-Rousseau style of pedagogy. The child was measured in terms of sectarian standards, it being assumed that the first step was to impress him with the truth that his very nature was sinful, and that it could be shrived only by having the mind centred always upon holy thoughts. The religion of the closet must be held above every pleasure. Yet Dr. Watts notices that such pleasures are increasing to an alarming state; that children are rebelling against Puritan principles. His sternness relents, in so far as he would allow children to play draughts and chess, and to amuse themselves with games which might instruct them in the rudiments of grammar and geometry.

Though there are not many who would discountenance his diatribe against the gaming table, the dangers besetting midnight revellers, and the freedom which results in immorality, one cannot but view with distrust the strictures which would turn girls into dowdy creatures and boys into prigs. The theoretical predecessors of Rousseau's Émile were the two creations of Dr. Watts,—Eugenio and Phronissa—his ideal children, combining those qualities which rob youth of all charm. Theirs must have been wearisome lives. The boy, we are told, "is an entertaining companion to the gay young gentlemen, his equals; and yet divines and philosophers take pleasure to have Eugenio amongst them." Dr. Watts never deigned to tell us what requirements Eugenio set for the staid divines, or whether he tried to get away from them. And Phronissa: she stands before us now, in attitude betokening detestation of the stage, and we hear her proclaiming the song and the dance as her meanest pleasures—talents not to be proud of!

Two points are worthy of note in Dr. Watts's book. Despite his many limitations which argued for piousness and for the composure of the youthful spirit; despite his disapproval of all exercise which might turn one's thoughts away from the prescribed paths, he was nevertheless a pleader in the cause of advance. For what he lays down as educational theory he would have parents hearken to; in his eyes the bringing up of youth is a sacred duty, involving obligations of a delicate nature. He would emphasise the responsibility of the Home; he would have parents eager to see the moral laws obeyed by their children. He would have education applied equally as well to girls as to boys; in fact, so Dr. Watts confesses, in tones as though he were making a great concession, the habit of reading is quite as important to the former as to the latter.

Dark as the days may seem in the lives of those children educated according to theories and tracts, the lighter recreations must have brightened moments unrecorded. Even John Locke (1632–1704), in his "Thoughts on Education" (1693), recommends besides the Psalter and the New Testament, Æsop and Reynard the Fox, as good food for infant minds. This was an excellent basis to start upon.

The two small volumes of "Divine Songs, Attempted in Easy Language for the Use of Children" [editions, New York: Mahlon Day; Cambridge: 1803] which I have examined, bear upon the fly-leaves tales recorded in uncertain handwriting. The one has, "To ——, a present from his Mamma"; the other, "—— his Book: If this should be lost and you should *fine*, Return to me, for it is *mine*."

"You will find here nothing that savours of party," says the poet in his foreword. "... As I have endeavoured to sink the language to the level of a child's understanding, and yet to keep it, if possible, above contempt, so I have designed to profit all, if possible, and to offend none."

Yet the usual theological doctrines reek from every page; there is much of the tenor of the "New England Primer" in the verses. The wonder is that with all their atmosphere of brimstone and sulphur, with all their effort to present *to* the child grown-up beliefs in simple doses, the poems still retain a spontaneity, a sweet, quaint simplicity that strike the sympathy, if they do not entirely appeal to the fancy. "His dreadful Majesty" is more suited to Milton than to a song; "How doth the little busy bee," though not yet in accord with the lyrist's pure, unfeigned delight in nature, is overtopping in childish appeal, "The eternal God will not disdain, To hear an infant cry." We pit an understanding of childhood's graces against that old-time theory of inherited ruin. There has been a revulsion of feeling which tends to bring the heart much nearer the soul, and to give to the nursery the sanctified love of good rather than the abiding fear of evil.

There is a picture in Lamb's "Books for Children" [ed. E. V. Lucas], showing the ark with the animals in their symmetrically built stalls. The clouds are rolling over the waters with as much substantial outline as though they were balls of cotton; there is interest for a child in the close examination of this graphic art, which is done with that surety as though the artist had been on the spot. The reproduction was made from Stackhouse's Bible, with which Mrs. Trimmer used to amuse her young folks on Sundays. Your wooden Noah's Ark, with the sticky animals, was built along the same lines. Dr. Watts's poems have been illustrated many times in similar conventional fashion. One cut in particular represented creation by a dreadful lion and a marvellous tiger, anatomically wonderful.

Though parts of the Bible have been paraphrased by Dr Watts as well as such can ever be done; though ducks and lambs and doves, symbols of simplicity, take one to the open, there is no breath of clover sweeping across the page. It is by such a beautiful cradle hymn as "Holy angels guard thy bed," which is to be treasured with Martin Luther's exquisite "Hymn to the Christ Child," that this poet deserves to be remembered.

Always the truest verse, the truest sentiment, the truest regard for children are detected in that retrospective tone—the eternal note of sadness, as Matthew Arnold phrases it—in which grown people speak of the realm of youth lost to them; not the sentimental stooping, not the condescending superiority,—but a yearning note brought about by the tragedy of growing up,—a yearning that passeth understanding, and that returns with every flash of the remembered child you were.

The Taylors of Ongar, the two sisters, Ann (1782–1866) and Jane (1783–1824), are the poets of the didactic era; they apply to verse the same characteristics Miss More introduced in her tracts—a sympathetic feeling, but a false tenderness. They are not doctrinal in their "Original Poems for Infant Minds," but are generally and genuinely ethical. Their attitude is different from that of Watts; they attempt to interpret feelings and impressions in terms of the child's own comprehension. But so far were they ruled by the customary requirements of their time, that they falsely endowed the juvenile mind with the power of correlating external beauty with its own virtuous possibilities. The simplicity of Jane's "The Violet" and "Thank you, Pretty Cow" is marked by an unnatural discrimination on the part of the children from whom such sentiments are supposed to flow; these defects detract from many a delicate verse deserving of better acquaintance than "Twinkle, twinkle, little star."

The Taylors wrote together for a number of years; they opened a field of interest in and kindness to animals; their verse abounds in the beginnings of a spontaneous love of nature. Their children troop past us, the industrious boy and the idle boy, the rich and the poor. They are not active children; their positions are fixed ones of contemplation, of inward communing, not of participation. Yet the sweet spirit predominates, and the simple words are not robbed of their purity and strength. However, their desire "to abridge every poetic freedom and figure" dragged them often into absurdities. This is the great danger in writing simple verse; unless its excellence is dominant, it shows its weakness; the outline of lyric beauty must have perfect symmetry; the slightest falsity in imagery, the slightest departure from consistency and truth, destroys the whole.[38]

Jane, when she was very small, used to edify her neighbours by preaching to them; this impulse found expression later in a series of hymns. Ann also composed religious songs which in quality are superior to those of her sister. The literary association of the two lasted until 1812, when Ann was sought in marriage by a Mr. Gilbert; this negotiation was consummated by letter before they had even met.

A further advance in the art of children's verse was made when William Blake (1757–1827) wrote his "Songs of Innocence," and infused into them a light spirit of grace and of joy. Strangely, he had difficulty in disposing of his poems; on this account, he determined to prepare the plates for them himself. The drawings which resulted proved to be some of his very best art work. Through his acquaintance with Godwin, he was employed to illustrate many of the books issuing from Mrs. Godwin's publishing house, and it has not yet been fully settled whether or not he made the original illustrations for the Lambs' "Tales from Shakespeare." He was employed to engrave the plates for Mary Wollstonecraft's translation of Salzmann's "Elements of Morality."

We detect in Blake's verses the apt blending of grown-up regard for childhood, with the ready response of childhood to grown-up love. By his exuberance, by his fancy, by his simple treatment he set a standard which is the same that dominates the best of Wordsworth and Christina Rossetti. Stevenson later carried forward the art, by adding thereto a touch as though youth, fearful of growing up, knew something of the heavy burden of man's estate. Thus does Blake express infant joy:

"I have no name:

I am but two days old."

What shall I call thee?

"I happy am,

Joy is my name."

Sweet joy befall thee.

The crystal clearness in such sentiment is born of our adult reverence. Again he makes the nurse in one of his poems sing:

"Then come home, my children, the sun is going down,

And the dews of night arise;

Come, come, leave off play, and let us away

Till the morning appears in the skies."

A child appreciates such mellow tones; there is no reaching down; the picture is distinct, reduced to its truest sentiment. It contains traceries of action, and fairest hints of beneficent nature. It gives a promise of to-morrow. There is no herding into the land of sleep. Let *us* away! Do you not feel the distinction of dignity in it, rather than "get *you* to bed"?

In Stevenson's verse the dominant note is retrospective; he returns to childhood with his quota of world experience; he slips into the youthful state, glad of being there once more, yet knowing what it all means to have to leave it again. Night fears and day joys flow through his lines:

Away down the river,

A hundred miles or more,

Other little children

Shall bring my boats ashore.

There is the preternatural strain of sadness in the make-up of youth; they like to discover in their elders those same characteristics they possess; they will creep to the strong arm of him who marvels as they do at the mystery of silent things. Such a one, even though grown-up, is worth while; he knows what it is to be in bed in summer with "the birds still hopping on the grass"; he knows what it is to be a child. Stevenson, the man, becomes the remembered boy.

The poetry for children that has lived is of that quality which appeals to the pristine sense of all that is fair and good and beautiful. Tender love, unfettered joy, protecting gentleness recognise no age; we, who are no longer young, look through the barred gates and up the gravel road, flanked by the dense freshness of green. Somewhere we hear the splash of water, far off we see the intense white of marble. Clinging to the iron bars outside, we watch the girl and boy, we count their footprints in the sand. They stoop to pick the violets as we stooped years ago; they look into the basin of clear water as we looked years ago. And then the path curves out of view. Here is where our appreciative contemplation of childhood becomes self-conscious; we cannot *see* the little ones doing what we did in years gone by. Perhaps this, perhaps that; we have our first *moral* doubt. Through the bars we call to the childhood of our memory; we call it to come back. The poet has but to sing of what he found beyond that bend when he was young, of the child he was, who once looked up at him from the clear depths; the boy and girl will creep down the gravel path again, they will marvel at what is told them of revolving suns, of the lost childhood, of the flight of birds, and of the shiver of grass. Let the poet but sing in true notes, making appeal to their imagery, giving them vigour in exchange for their responsiveness, and understanding in exchange for their trust; they will return, even to the iron gate, and take him by the hand. This is what it means to be the laureate of childhood.

V. CHARLES AND MARY LAMB; THE GODWINS.

A story is told of Charles Lamb which, in view of actual facts, one must necessarily disbelieve. It is to the effect that, dining out one evening, he heard in an adjoining room the noise of many children. With his glass filled, he rose from his chair and drank the toast, "Here's to the health of good King Herod." Instinctively, those familiar with Elia will recollect his "Dream Children," and wonder how any critic could reconcile the two attitudes. Lamb had an abiding love for young people and a keen understanding of their natures.

As writers of juvenile literature, Charles (1775–1834) and Mary (1765–1847) Lamb might never have been known, had it not been for William Godwin (1756–1836) and his second wife. The two began a publishing business, in 1805, under the firm name of M. J. Godwin and Company. The only details that concern us are those which began and ended with the Lambs and their work. Godwin, himself, under the pseudonym of Baldwin, turned out literary productions of various kinds. But though, during one period, there was every sign of a flourishing trade, by 1822 the business was bankrupt.

The Lambs regarded their writings for children as pot-boilers; letters from them abound with such confessions. But it was in their natures to treat their work lovingly; their own personalities entered the text; they drew generously upon themselves; and so their children's books are filled with their own experiences, and are, in many respects, as autobiographical as the "Essays of Elia." Mary undertook by far the larger number of the volumes which are usually accredited to her brother; in fact, wherever the two collaborated, Lamb occupied a secondary place.

The following list indicates the division of labour:

THE KING AND QUEEN OF HEARTS, 1805. Lamb's first juvenile work.

TALES FROM SHAKESPEARE, 1807. Lamb wrote to Manning, May 10, 1806: "I have done 'Othello' and 'Macbeth,' and mean to do all the tragedies. I think it will be popular among the little people, besides money."

ADVENTURES OF ULYSSES, 1808. "Intended," as Lamb told Manning, "to be an introduction to the reading of Telemachus; it is done out of the 'Odyssey,' not from the Greek. I would not mislead you; nor yet from Pope's 'Odyssey,' but from an older translation of one Chapman. The 'Shakespeare Tales' suggested doing it." Lamb's delight in Chapman was as unalloyed as that of Keats.

MRS. LEICESTER'S SCHOOL, 1809. Issued anonymously, hence commonly ascribed to Lamb. The greater part of the work belongs to Mary; it seems to have been her idea originally. Lamb to Barton, January 23, 1824: "My Sister's part in the Leicester School (about two-thirds) was purely her own; as it was (to the same quantity) in the Shakespeare Tales which bear my name. I wrote only the Witch Aunt, the First Going to Church, and the final story about a little Indian Girl in a Ship."

POETRY FOR CHILDREN, 1809. Lamb claimed about one-third of the book as his own. Mr. Lucas believes that Mrs. Godwin issued these verses to compete with the Taylors and Adelaide O'Keeffe.

PRINCE DORUS OR FLATTERY PUT OUT OF COUNTENANCE, 1811. Robinson wrote: "I this year tried to persuade him [Lamb] to make a new version of the old Tale of Reynard the Fox. He said he was sure it would not succeed—sense for humour, said L., is extinct." "Prince Dorus" was done instead.

BEAUTY AND THE BEAST, 1811. Authorship doubtful.

There is something keenly pathetic in noting the brother and sister at work in the interests of children, hoping to add to their yearly income—sitting down together and thinking out conceptions for their juvenile poems and stories. Mary Lamb reveals, by those smaller elements in her prose, a keener discernment of what a child's book should be; she is far more successful than her brother in entering into the spirit of the little lives she writes about, while Lamb himself is happiest in his touches where he is handling the literary subjects.[39] But on the whole, Lamb's style was not suited to the making of children's books. We see them, while writing the Shakespeare Tales, seated at one table, "an old literary Darby and Joan," Mary tells Sarah Stoddart, "I taking snuff and he groaning all the while, and saying he can make nothing of it, which he always says till he has finished, and then he finds out he has made something of it...."

Mrs. Godwin doubtless conceived her system of advertising direct from Newbery; in the story of "Emily Barton," which forms part of "Mrs. Leicester's School," Mary Lamb tells how Emily's papa ordered the coachman to drive to the Juvenile Library in Skinner street [No. 41], where seven books were bought, "and the lady in the shop persuaded him to take more, but mamma said that was quite enough at present."

By this, the Lambs indicated a willingness to accord with any business suggestions which might further the interests of the Godwins; nevertheless, they were not so bound that they could not act independently. And, in view of the fact that Lamb disliked Mrs. Godwin, there was a certain graciousness revealed in the concessions they did make from time to time. Elia was to discover that Godwin had his eye alert for any unnecessary element of cruelty which might creep into their books for children. When the publishers were given the manuscript of "Ulysses," Godwin wrote a letter to Lamb, on March 10, 1808, which, with the answer, is worth quoting, since the attitude is one to be considered by all writers and by all library custodians.

DEAR LAMB:

I address you with all humility, because I know you to be *tenax propositi*. Hear me, I entreat you, with patience.

It is strange with what different feelings an author and a bookseller look at the same manuscript. I know this by experience: I was an author, I am a bookseller. The author thinks what will conduce to his honour; the bookseller, what will cause his commodities to sell.

You, or some other wise man, I have heard to say [it was Johnson]: It is children that read children's books, when they are read, but it is parents that choose them. The critical thought of the tradesman puts itself therefore into the place of the parent, and what the parent will condemn.

We live in squeamish days. Amid the beauties of your manuscript, of which no man can think more highly than I do, what will the squeamish say to such expressions as these, 'devoured their limbs, yet warm and trembling, lapping the blood,' page 10. Or to the giant's vomit, page 14, or to the minute and shocking description of the extinguishing the giant's eye in the page following. You, I dare say, have no formed plan of excluding the female sex from among your readers, and I, as a bookseller, must consider that, if you have, you exclude one half of the human species.

Nothing is more easy than to modify these things if you please, and nothing, I think, is more indispensable....

The main argument here stated daily confronts the librarian and the author; it is one so often over-considered, that in its wake it leaves a diluted literature, mild in expression, faint in impression, weak in situation, and lacking in colour. There is a certain literary style that, through zealous regard for refinement, misses the rugged vitality which marks the old-time story, and which constitutes its chief hold upon life. On the other hand, children need very little stimulation, provided it is virile, to set them in active accord; and it is wise for publishers to consider the omissions of those unnecessary details, situations, or actions, without which the story is in no way harmed. But to curtail or to dilute the full meaning, to give a part for the whole, has resulted in producing so many versions of the same tale or legend as to make the young reader doubt which is the correct one; and in most cases leave in him no desire to turn to the original source. On your library shelves, are you to have five or six versions of the same story, issued by as many rival publishing houses, or are you to discard them all and take only that one which is *nearest* the original in spirit and in general excellence?

Lamb here brushed against the problem of writing for the popular taste. This is how he met it:

MARCH 11, 1808.

DEAR GODWIN:

The giant's vomit was perfectly nauseous, and I am glad you pointed it out. I have removed the objection. To the other passages I can find no objection but what you may bring to numberless passages besides, such as of Scylla snatching up the six men, etc.,—that is to say, they are lively images of *shocking* things. If you want a book which is not occasionally to *shock*, you should not have thought of a tale which is so full of anthropophagi and wonders. I cannot alter these things without enervating the Book, and I will not alter them if the penalty should be that you and all the London booksellers should refuse it. But speaking as author to author, I must say that I think *the terrible* in those two passages seems to me so much to preponderate over the nauseous as to make them rather fine than disgusting. [Remember, this is spoken by one who in youth was sensitive and whose feelings are graphically set forth in "Witches, and Other Night Fears."]... I only say that I will not consent to alter such passages, which I know to be some of the best in the book. As an author, I say to you, an author, Touch not my work. As to a bookseller I say, Take the work, such as it is, or refuse it. You are free to refuse it as when we first talked of it. As to a friend I say, Don't plague yourself and me with nonsensical objections. I assure you I will not alter one more word.

Lamb's critical genius often showed remarkable subtlety in the fine distinctions drawn between shades of effect which are produced by art. He established, through his careful analyses, an almost new critical attitude toward Shakespeare; and, in days when psychology as a study was unknown, when people witnessed the different phases of emotional life and judged them before formulæ were invented by which to test them scientifically, he saw, with rare discrimination, the part that the spiritual value of literature was to play in the development of culture. He here weighs in the balance a fine terror with a nauseous scene; such a difference presupposes a clear insight into the story and a power to arrive at the full meaning at once; it infers an instinctive knowledge of the whole gamut of possible effects. Lamb's plea to Godwin is the plea of the man who would rather keep a child in the green fields than have him spend his time on wishy-washy matter.

The whole discussion resolves itself into the question: How much of the brute element, in which early literature abounds, is to be given to children? Shall they be made to fear unnecessarily, shall the ugly phases of life be allowed, simply because they come through the ages stamped as classic? All due consideration must be paid to the sensitiveness of childhood; but in what manner? Not by catering to it, not by eliminating the cause from the story without at the same time seeking to strengthen the inherent weakness of the child. Dr. Felix Adler[40] would remove from our folk-lore all the excrescences that denote a false superstition and that create prejudice of any kind; he would have bad stepmothers taken from the fairy tales, because an unjust hatred for a class is encouraged; he would prune away whatever is of no ornamental or ethical value. Assuredly it is best, as Dr. Adler points out, "to eliminate ... whatever is merely a relic of ancient animism." Mr. Howells believes that it is our pedant pride which perpetuates the beast man in our classics, and it is true that some of our literature has lived in spite of that characteristic, and not because of it. But who is to point this beast man out for us, who is to judge whether this or that corrupts, who to eliminate and who to recreate? The classics would have to be rewritten whenever there was a shift in moral viewpoint.

A mushroom growth of story-writers, those who "tame" our fairy tales, who dilute fancy with sentimentalism, and who retell badly what has been told surpassing well, threatens to choke the flower. It is not the beast man in classic literature we have to fear so much as the small man of letters, enthused by the educational idea, who rewrites to order, and does not put into his text any of the invigorating spirit which marks all truly great literature. We have always to return to the ultimate goal, to the final court of appeal. If there is too much brutal strength in a story intended for children, it had best be read or told to them, rather than place in their hands what is not literature but the mere husk.

Such a letter as Lamb wrote to Godwin leads us to feel that at times misgivings seized him as to his own mutilation of Homer and of his much-beloved Chapman. But such hesitancy is the exception and not the rule to-day.

As poets for children the Lambs strike their most artificial note; the verses are forced and written according to prescribed formulæ. There is a mechanical effort in them to appear youthful, as though before setting to the task—for so the two called it—a memorandum of childish deeds and thoughts and expressions had been drawn up, from which each was to extract inspiration. But inspiration is sorely lacking; to most of the poems you can apply the stigma of "old maids" children; there is little that is naturally playful or spontaneously appealing in sentiment. Such lines as "Crumbs to the Birds" are unaffected and simple, and the paraphrase "On the Lord's Prayer" aptly interpretative. But on the whole, the verses are stilted; the feeling in them comes not from the authors so much as it indicates how carefully it was thought out by them. We find Lamb making excuses to Coleridge in June, 1809: "Our little poems are ... humble, but they have no name. You must read them, remembering they were task-work; and perhaps you will admire the number of subjects, all of children, picked out by an old bachelor and an old maid. Many parents would not have found so many."

It is this utmost sincerity and such a naïve confession which make Charles Lamb one of the most lovable figures in English literature.

Bibliographical Note

LUCAS, E. V.—Old-Fashioned Tales. Selected by. London, Wells, Gardner, Darton & Co.; New York, Stokes.

LUCAS, E. V.—Forgotten Tales of Long Ago. Selected by. London, Wells, Gardner, Darton & Co.; New York, Stokes, 1906.

MORLEY, JOHN—Jean Jacques Rousseau. Macmillan.

ROUSSEAU, JEAN JACQUES—Émile; or, Treatise on Education. Abridged and Translated by W. H. Payne. (International Educational Series.) New York, Appleton, 1893.

DE GENLIS, COMTESSE, As an Educator. *Nation*, 73:183 (Sept. 5, '01).

DE GENLIS, COUNTESS, Memoirs of the. Illustrative of the History of the 18th and 19th Century. Written by herself. (2 vols.) [English translation.] New York, Wilder & Campbell, 1825.

DE GENLIS, COMTESSE—Théâtre d'Éducation. (5 vols.) Paris, 1825.

DE GENLIS, COMTESSE—Adelaide and Theodore. Letters on Education,—containing all the principles relative to three different plans of education; to that of princes, and to those of young persons of both sexes. Translated from the French. (3 vols.) London, 1788.

BERQUIN, ARNAUD—The Children's Friend, Being a Selection from the Works of. Montrose, 1798.

BERQUIN, ARNAUD—L'Ami des Enfants. Paris, 1792.

EDGEWORTH, MARIA—The Parent's Assistant; or, Stories for Children. (3 vols.)

EDGEWORTH, MARIA, AND RICHARD LOVELL—Practical Education. (1st American ed., 2 vols.) New York, 1801.

EDGEWORTH, RICHARD LOVELL, Memoirs of. Begun by himself and concluded by his daughter, Maria Edgeworth. (2 vols.) London, Hunter, 1820.

HARE, AUGUSTUS J. C.—Life and Letters of Maria Edgeworth. (2 vols.) London, Arnold, 1894.

EDGEWORTH, MARIA—Tales from. With an Introduction by Austin Dobson. New York, Stokes, $1.50.

PANCOAST, H. S.—Forgotten Patriot. *Atlantic*, 91:758 (June, '03).

RAY, A. C.—Philosopher's Wooing. *Book-buyer*, 24:287 (May, '02).

FYVIE, JOHN—Literary Eccentricities. London, Constable, 1906. [*Vide* p. 35: The author of "Sandford and Merton."]

DAY, THOMAS—Life of. (In the British Poets, Vol. lviii.) [By R. A. Davenport, Esq.]

DAY, THOMAS—Sandford and Merton. London, George Routledge & Sons, 3s. 6d.

BARBAULD, ANNA LETITIA—A Legacy for Young Ladies.... By the late Mrs. B. London, 1826. [Morality leaps from every page, but the book is agreeably written.]

BARBAULD AND AIKIN—Evenings at Home. London, Routledge, 2s. 6d.

MURCH, JEROM—Mrs. Barbauld and Her Contemporaries: Sketches of Some Eminent Literary and Scientific English Women. London, Longmans, 1877. [*Vide* also Memoir and Letters, ed. Grace A. Ellis; also Memoir by Anna Letitia LeBreton.]

BARBAULD, MRS.—Hymns in Prose. London, Routledge, 2s.

RAIKES, ROBERT—The Man and His Work. Biographical Notes Collected by Josiah Harris. Unpublished Letters by Robert Raikes. Letters from the Raikes family. Opinions on Influence of Sunday Schools. (Specially Contributed.) Ed. J. Henry Harris. Introduction by Dean Farrar, D.D. Bristol, London. [Illustrated; frontispiece of Raikes.]

RAIKES, ROBERT—Memoir of the Founder of Sunday Schools. [Pamphlet.] G. Webster. Nottingham, 1873.

TRIMMER, MRS.—Some Account of the Life and Writings of, with original letters, and meditations and prayers, selected from her Journal. London, 1825.

TRIMMER, MRS. SARAH—The History of the Robins. (Ed. Edward Everett Hale.) Heath, 1903. [In its day, this book was illustrated by many well-known artists.]

MORE, HANNAH, Life of. [Famous Women Series.] Charlotte M. Yonge. Boston, Roberts, 1890.

MORE, HANNAH, Life of, with Notices of her Sisters. Henry Thompson, M.A. (2 vols.) Philadelphia, Carey and Hart, 1838.

MORE, HANNAH, The Works of. (1st Complete American ed.) Harper, 1852. [*Vide* also Memoirs by W. Roberts and Mrs. H. C. Knight; Mrs. Elwood's Memoirs of Literary Ladies; *Monthly Review*, Feb., 1809; April, 1813, Feb., 1820. *Vide* London: Nurimo, for publication of many of Miss More's, Mrs. Sherwood's and Jane Taylor's stories.]

BLAKE, WILLIAM, The Lyric Poems of. Ed. John Sampson. Oxford, Clarendon Press, 1905.

BLAKE, WILLIAM, The Works of. Ed. E. J. Ellis and William Butler Yeats. (3 vols.) London, 1893.

LAMB, CHARLES AND MARY—Works. Ed. E. V. Lucas. (Putnam.) Works. Ed. Canon Ainger. (Macmillan.)

TAYLOR, ANN AND JANE—The "Original Poems" and Others. Ed. E. V. Lucas. New York, Stokes, $1.50.

TAYLOR, JANE AND ANN—Greedy Dick, and Other Stories in Verse. Stokes, $0.50.

WATTS, DR. ISAAC—London, Houlston. The same publishing house prints volumes by Mrs. Sherwood, Mrs. Cameron, Miss Edgeworth, H. Martineau, the Taylors, etc.

WATTS, DR. ISAAC—Divine and Moral Songs. London, Elkin Mathews, 1s. 6d. net.

FOOTNOTES

[31] She is the author of a remarkably bold "Manuel du Voyageur" en Six Langues. Paris, Barrois, 1810. Framed to meet every conceivable occasion.

[32] Day was honest in his intentions, however mistaken his policy may have been. Sabrina finally married a Mr. Bicknell, who willingly allowed her to accept support, meagre as it was, from Day.

[33] Mrs. Godwin [Mary Wollstonecraft] (1759–1797) began, as an exercise, to translate "The Elements of Morality, for the Use of Children," written by the Reverend Christian Gotthilf Salzmann (1744–1811), who won no small renown for the excellence of his school, founded upon the principles set down by Rousseau. "The design of this book," says the worthy master, "is to give birth to what we call a good disposition in children." The chief delight of the 1782 edition, published in three volumes, are the copperplates which represent in the most graphic way, by pose, gesture, expression, and caption, all the ills that juvenile flesh is heir to. No one, after having once viewed the poor little figure seated on a most forbidding-looking sofa, can quite resist the pangs of sympathy over his exclamation: "How sad is life without a friend!" Life is indeed a direful wilderness of trials and vexations. The prismatic colors of one's years shrivel up before such wickedness as is expressed by the picture "I hate you!" And yet how simple is the remedy for a boy's bad disposition, according to the Reverend Mr. Salzmann! "Teach him," so the philosopher argues in his preface, "that envy is the vexation which is felt at seeing the happiness of others: you will have given him a just idea of it; but shew him its dreadful effects, in the example of Hannah in chap. 29, vol. II, who was so tormented by this corroding passion, at her sister's wedding, that she could neither eat, drink, nor sleep, and was so far carried away by it as to embitter her innocent sister's pleasure; this representation has determined the child's disposition—he will hate envy." Elements of Morality ... Translated from the German.... 3d ed. (3 vols.) London, 1782.

[34] Charles Lamb has recorded his vivid impressions of this book in "Witches and Other Night Fears."

[35] It is interesting to note the longevity of many of the women writers of this period. Both Miss Edgeworth and Mrs. Barbauld died in their eighty-second year, while Miss More reached the ripe age of eighty-eight. Mrs. Trimmer, nearing seventy, was thus comparatively young at the time of her death. A glimpse of Miss More at seventy-nine is left in the reminiscences of the original Peter Parley, who visited her, *circa* 1823, much as a devout pilgrim would make a special journey. He wrote: "She was small and wasted away. Her attire was of dark-red bombazine, made loose like a dressing-gown. Her eyes were black and penetrating, her face glowing with cheerfulness, through a lace-work of wrinkles. Her head-dress was a modification of the coiffure of her earlier days—the hair being slightly frizzled, and lightly powdered, yet the whole group of moderate dimensions."

[36] *Vide* the lay sermon by Samuel McCord Crothers, "The Colonel in the Theological Seminary."—*Atlantic*, June, 1907. Also Emerson's essay on "Spiritual Laws."

[37] *Vide* Miss Strickland's "Lives of the Seven Bishops."

[38] For Jane Taylor, *vide* "Contributions of Q Q;" "Essays in Rhymes on Morals and Planners." For Ann Taylor, *vide* "Hymns for Infant Schools."

[39] Frederic Harrison, in his "The Choice of Books," (Macmillan, 1886) writes:

"Poor Lamb has not a little to answer for, in the revived relish for garbage unearthed from old theatrical dung-heaps. Be it just or earnest, I have little patience with the Elia-tic philosophy of the frivolous. Why do we still suffer the traditional hypocrisy about the dignity of literature,—literature I mean, in the gross, which includes about equal parts of what is useful and what is useless? Why are books as books, writers as writers, readers as readers, meritorious, apart from any good in them, or anything that we can get from them?"

[40] The reader is referred to "The Moral Instruction of Children," by Felix Adler, New York: Appleton, 1892. Besides considering the use to be made of fairy tales, fables, and Bible stories, the author discusses fully the elements in the Odyssey and the Iliad which are valuable adjuncts in moral training.

IV.
CONCERNING NOW AND THEN

Ce que je vois alors dans ce jardin, c'est un petit bonhomme qui, les mains dans les poches et sa gibecière au dos, s'en va au collège en sautillant comme un moineau. Ma pensée seule le voit; car ce petit bonhomme est une ombre; c'est l'ombre du moi que j'étais il y a vingt-cinq ans. Vraiment, il m'intéresse, ce petit: quand il existait, je ne me souciais guère de lui; mais, maintenant qu'il n'est plus, je l'aime bien. Il valait mieux, en somme, que les autres moi que j'ai eus après avoir perdu celui-là. Il était bien étourdi; mais il n'était pas méchant et je dois lui; rendre cette justice qu'il ne m'a pas laissé un seul mauvais souvenir; c'est un innocent que j'ai perdu: il est bien naturel que je le regrette; il est bien naturel que je le voie en pensée et que mon esprit s'amuse à ranimer son souvenir.... Tout ce qu'il voyait alors, je le vois aujourd'hui. C'est le même ciel et la même terre; les choses ont leur âme d'autrefois, leur âme qui m'égaye et m'attriste, et me trouble; lui seul n'est plus.—Anatole France, in "Le Livre de mon Ami."

"I prefer the little girls and boys ... that come as you call them, fair or dark, in green ribbons or blue. I like making cowslip fields grow and apple-trees bloom at a moment's notice. That is what it is, you see, to have gone through life with an enchanted land ever beside you...."—Kate Greenaway to Ruskin.

I. THE ENGLISH SIDE.

Whatever change in children's literature was now to take place was due entirely to the increasing importance of elementary education. A long while was to elapse before the author was wholly freed from the idea that situations could be dealt with, apart from any overbearing *morale*, and even then he found himself constrained to meet the problem of giving information—of teaching instead of preaching.

The interest in external nature, the desire to explain phenomena according to the dictates of belief, infused a new element into authorship for young people. But those writers brought to meet this latent stirring of the scientific spirit all the harness of the old régime. First they thought that they could explain the evident by parables, but they found that fact was too particular for generalisations, and the child mind too immature for such symbol. Then they attempted to define natural objects from a childish plane, making silly statements take the place of truth. They soon became aware that their simple style had to deal with a set of details that could not be sentimentalised.

The truth of the matter is that a new impulse was started; the national spirit began to move toward a more democratic goal; the rank and file began to look beyond the narrow hill and dale; women sought wider spheres; the poor demanded constitutional rights; energy began to stir from underneath. The word *modern* was in every one's mind. The old order changeth, giving place to new. The child's intellect must be furnished with food for its growth; Rousseau's doctrine of "back to nature" was found not to have worked; it was realised that special training must begin early for all the walks of life. Carlyle was pleading for a *public* library, education was widening its sphere.

In the preceding pages, we have tried to establish a continuous line of development in children's books through several centuries; upon such a foundation the English story and the American story of to-day are based. The table of English writers on page 147 contains names of minor importance, but still forming a part of the past history—foreshadowers of the new era. For therein you will discover that juvenile literature first begins to show signs of differing from adult literature only in its power; that where Macaulay tells the story of England in terms of maturity, Miss Strickland, Lady Callcott, Miss Tytler, and Miss Yonge adopt a descending scale. Where children were wont to act in accord with the catechism, they are now made to feel an interest in their surroundings. Mrs. Marcet writes for them "talks" on chemistry and political economy, Mrs. Wakefield on botany and insects. The extension of schools meant that literature must be supplied those schools; writers were encouraged in the same way that Miss More was prompted to produce her "Repository Tracts." Grammars and histories began to flood the market, and in the wake of Scott's novels, taking into consideration the fact that books were being written for the purpose of information, the child's historical story was a natural consequence. Thus we discover the connection between "Waverley" and Henty. The death-blow to fairy tales in England, brought about by the didactic writers, resulted in a deplorable lack of imaginative literature for children, until a German influence, around 1840–1850, began to take effect, and the Grimms' Household Tales afforded a new impulse.[41] Mrs. Gatty, author of the famous "Parables of Nature," deigned to rejoice over the classic nonsense of Lewis Carroll. The line of descent can be drawn from Perrault to Grimm, from Grimm to Andrew Lang's rainbow series of folk-lore.

The table is intended to do no more than indicate the gradual manner in which this break took effect. The student who would treat the evolution fully will find it necessary to place side by side with his discussion of individual books for young people, a full explanation of those social changes in English history which are the chief causes of the changes in English literature. Children's books are subject to just those modifications which take place in the beliefs, the knowledge, and the aspirations of the adult person. The difference between the two is one of intensity and not of kind. The student will discover, after a study of the development of the common school, how and why the educational impulse dominated over all elements of pure imagination; how the retelling craze, given a large literary sanction by such a writer as Lamb, and so excellently upheld by Charles Kingsley, lost caste when brought within compass of the text-book. He will finally see how this educational pest has overrun America to a far greater extent than England, to the detriment of much that is worthy and of much which should by rights be made to constitute a children's reading heritage.

ENGLISH TABLE

MRS. PRISCILLA WAKEFIELD. 1751–1832. Member of Society of Friends; philanthropic work among the poor. Author: Juvenile Anecdotes; Juvenile Travellers; Conversations; Introduction to Botany; Introduction to Insects; Present Condition of Female Sex, with Suggestions for Its Improvement; Life of William Penn. Reference: D. N. B.[42]

FRANCES BURNEY (MADAME D'ARBLAY). 1752–1840. Reference: D. N. B.

WILLIAM FORDYCE MAVOR. 1758–1837. Ed. 1799, juvenile periodical for Walker, Newbery. Reference: D. N. B.

JOANNA BAILLIE. 1762–1851. Work among the poor made her known as Lady Bountiful. Reference: D. N. B.

JEREMIAH JOYCE. 1763–1816. Author: Lectures on the Microscope.

MRS. JANE MARCET. 1769–1858. Macaulay wrote: "Every girl who has read Mrs. Marcet's little dialogues on political economy could teach Montague or Walpole many fine lessons in finance." Author: Scientific text-books; Conversations on Chemistry intended for the Female Sex; Conversations on Political Economy, imitated by Harriet Martineau in her Illustrations of Political Economy. Reference: D. N. B.

MRS. BARBARA HOFLAND. 1770–1844. Imitated the Edgeworth style. Author: Emily; The Son of a Genius; Tales of a Manor; Young Crusoe. Reference: D. N. B.

MRS. MARY MARTHA SHERWOOD. 1775–1851. Stories and tracts evangelical in tone. With her sister, Mrs. Cameron, invented a type of story for rich and for poor. Author: The Fairchild Family (intended for the middle classes); Little Henry and His Bearer. Reference: *New Review* (May 18, 1843); Life of Mrs. Sherwood by her daughter; D. N. B. An edition of The Fairchild Family, New York, Stokes, $1.50.

JANE PORTER. 1776–1850. Reference: D. N. B.

MARIA HACK. 1778–1844. Quaker parentage. A believer in the "walk" species of literature. Author: Winter Evenings, or Tales of Travellers; First Lessons in English Grammar; Harry Beaufoy, or the Pupil of Nature. Reference: D. N. B.

MRS. ELIZABETH PENROSE. 1780–1837. Pseud. Mrs. Markham. Daughter of a rector. One critic wrote: "Mrs. Penrose adapted her history to what she considered the needs of the young, and omitted scenes of cruelty and fraud, as hurtful to children, and party politics after the Revolution as too complicated for them to learn." Author: Began school histories in 1823; these were brought up to date afterward by Mary Howitt. Moral Tales and Sermons for Children. Reference: D. N. B.

JOHN WILSON CROKER. 1780–1857. One of the founders of the *Quarterly Review*; reviewed abusively Keats's Endymion. Author: Stories from the History of England, 1817, which supplied Scott with the idea for his Tales of a Grandfather; Irish Tales. Reference: Jenning's Diaries and Correspondence of Croker (London, 1884); Internat. Encyclo.

LADY MARIA CALLCOTT. 1785–1842. Author: Little Arthur's History of England. Reference: D. N. B.

MARY RUSSELL MITFORD. 1787–1855. Careful detail of description, akin to Dutch style of painting. Author: Tragedies; Village Stories; Juvenile Spectator. She was among the first women to adopt writing as a profession. Miss Yonge speaks of her "writing so deliciously of children," but she "could not write for them." Reference: D. N. B.; Recollections; Letters.

AGNES STRICKLAND. 1796–1874. "With the exception of Jane Porter, whom she visited at Bristol, and with whom she carried on a frequent correspondence, and a casual meeting with Macaulay, whom she found congenial, she came little in contact with the authors of the day." Author: Lives of the Queens of England; Two Rival Crusoes. [Note the hybrid type of story that sprung up around the real Robinson Crusoe.] Edited Fisher's Juvenile Scrap Book, 1837–1839. Reference: D. N. B.

MRS. MAY SEWELL. 1797–1884. Left Society of Friends for the Church of England. Wrote homely ballads. *Vide* daughter, Anna Sewell. Author: Her ballad, Mother's Last Words, circulated about 1,088,000 copies when it first appeared. Reference: Mod. Biog.

MARY HOWITT. 1799–1888. Authorship linked with that of her husband. In 1837 began writing children's stories and poems. Her daughter, Anna Mary, also was a writer of children's books. Author: Translator of Fredrika Bremer's novels; editor, Fisher's Drawingroom Scrap Book. Reference: Reminiscences of My Later Life (*Good Words*, 1886); D. N. B.

CATHERINE SINCLAIR. 1800–1864. Fourth daughter of Sir John Sinclair. Her work considered the beginning of the modern spirit. A friend of Scott. Author: Holiday House; Modern Accomplishment; Modern Society; Modern Flirtations. Reference: A Brief Tribute to C. S. (Pamphlet); D. N. B.

G. P. R. JAMES. 1801–1860. Influenced by Scott and encouraged by Irving. Thackeray parodied him in Barbazure, by G. P. R. Jeames, Esq., in Novels by Eminent Hands; also in Book of Snobs (chaps. ii and xvi). Author of a long list of novels.

HARRIET MARTINEAU. 1802–1876. Reference: D. N. B.

MRS. MARGARET SCOTT GATTY. 1809–1873. She was forty-two before she began to publish. *Vide* Ewing. Author: Aunt Judy Tales; Parables of Nature; 1866—*Aunt Judy Magazine* (monthly), continued after her death, with her daughter as editor; stopped in 1885. Reference: Life in ed. Parables (Everyman's Library); *Illustrated London News*, Oct. 18, 1873; *Athenæum*, Oct. 11, 1873, p. 464; D. N. B.

ANNA SEWELL. 1820–1878. Author: Black Beauty (1877). Reference: D. N. B.

CHARLOTTE M. YONGE. 1823-. Author: Heir of Redclyffe; The Kings of England; The Chaplet of Pearls.

MRS. MARY LOUISA WHATELEY. 1824–1889. Went to Cairo and lived from 1861–1889, where she had a Moslem school. Wrote chiefly about Egypt. Fairy tale influence. Author: Reverses; or, the Fairfax Family. Reference: Hays' Women of To-day; London *Times* (March 12, 1889).

MRS. DINAH MARIA MULOCK CRAIK. 1826–1887. Pseudo-fairy tale writer. Author: Adventures of a Brownie, etc.

JULIANA HORATIO EWING. 1841–1885. Reference: J. H. Ewing and Her Books, by Horatia K. T. Gatty; D. N. B.

ANN FRASER TYTLER. Daughter of Alexander Fraser Tytler, Lord Woodhouselel. Author: Leila on the Island; Leila in England; Leila at Home.

II. THE AMERICAN SIDE.

As for the American phase of the subject, we have already indicated three stages by which the Colonial or Revolutionary reader was given his "New England Primer," his "Mother Goose," and his Thomas books obtained directly from Newbery of England. The whole intellectual activity was in the hands of the clergy; even the governing body pretended to be God-fearing men, and were prone to listen to the dictates of the ministry. The austere demands of the Puritan Sunday, more than anything else, caused the writing of religious books, and so firm a hold did the Sabbath *genre* of literature take, that, in 1870, it was still in full sway, and even now exists to a limited extent. The history of education in America for a long while has to do with denominational schools, and teaching was largely left in the hands of the clergy. So that we shall find our early writer of "juveniles" either a man of the church, or his wife; prompted solely by the desire to supply that character of story which would fitly harmonise with the sanctity of Sunday, rather than with the true excellence of all days. If, in the school, a book was needed, it was far better to write one than to trust to others for what might turn out to be heretical.[43] The Rev. Jedidiah Morse began his literary career in the capacity of teacher; Noah Webster's idea was at first to prepare a treatise on grammar which could be used in the schools. These two were the most scientific thinkers of their period. The list on page 158, indicating but a few of the forgotten and only faintly remembered authors of early days, fairly well represents the general trend; in the writing done, there were the same morals, the similar luckless children, subject to the same thin sentiment of piety and rectitude as we discovered holding sway in England for nearly two centuries. The name of Peter Parley is no longer familiar to children, and a crusade is fast being formed against the Jacob Abbott class of book. The type of writer was the kind that debated for or against slavery in terms of the Bible. The Puritan soil was rich for the rapid growth of the Hannah More seed, and no one assisted in sowing it to greater extent than Samuel G. Goodrich (1793–1860). He may symbolise for us the reading child in New England at the beginning of the nineteenth century; his training, his daily pursuits, as told in his autobiography, supply pages of invaluable social colour.[44]

"It is difficult," so he says, "... in this era of literary affluence, almost amounting to surfeit, to conceive of the poverty of books suited to children in the days of which I write. Except the New England Primer—the main contents of which were the Westminster Catechism—and some rhymes, embellished with hideous cuts of Adam's Fall, in which 'we sinned all'; the apostle and a cock crowing at his side, to show that 'Peter denies his Lord and cries'; Nebuchadnezzar crawling about like a hog, the bristles sticking out of his back, and the like—I remember none that were in general use among my companions. When I was about ten years old, my father brought from Hartford 'Gaffer Ginger,' 'Goody Two Shoes,' and some of the rhymes and jingles now collected under the name of 'Mother Goose,' with perhaps a few other toy books of that day. These were a revelation. Of course I read them, but I must add, with no relish."

The confession follows that when he was given "Red Riding Hood," he was filled with contempt; and in this spirit he condemns such nonsense as "hie diddle diddle," which is not fit for Christian parents to use. He found some considerable pleasure in "Robinson Crusoe," but it was not until he met with Miss Hannah More's tracts that he might be said to have enjoyed with relish any book at all.

Thus his reading tastes foreshadowed his literary activity. When he turned writer, he aimed for the style which distinguishes Mary Howitt, Mrs. Hofland, and Miss Strickland; he disclaimed any interest in the nursery book that was unreasonable and untruthful, for so he considered most of the stories of fancy. In his books, his desire was chiefly "to feed the young mind upon things wholesome and pure, instead of things monstrous, false, and pestilent.... In short, that the element of nursery books should consist of beauty instead of deformity, goodness instead of wickedness, decency instead of vulgarity." In this manner, the mould of the Peter Parley tales was shaped. Goodrich at first adopted no philosophy of construction, so he says; he aimed to tell his story as he would have spoken it to a group of boys. But after a while, a strong sense of the child's gradual growth took hold of him; he recognised psychological stages, and he saw that, as in teaching, his books must consider that children's "first ideas are simple and single, and formed of images of things palpable to the senses."

While on a visit to England in 1823—the memorable time he met Miss More—he turned his attention to what was being accomplished there in popular education for children. After investigation, he thus wrote:

"Did not children love truth? If so, was it necessary to feed them on fiction? Could not history, natural history, geography, biography become the elements of juvenile works, in place of fairies and giants, and mere monsters of the imagination? These were the inquiries that from this time filled my mind."

Under such conditions Peter Parley was born, and reborn, and overborn; battles were waged for and against him, just as they have only recently been waged for and against the Elsie books. But no sooner was Peter Parley identified with a definite person than Mr. Goodrich's trials began. He became a victim of the imperfect copyright system; he found his tales being pirated in England. And as fast as he would settle one difficulty, another would arise; spurious Parleys came to light, conflicting with his sales. It was the case of Goodrich *alias* Kettell, *alias* Mogridge, *alias* Martin, and many more beside. In fact, a writer, considering the life of William Martin (1801–1867), quotes a statement to the effect that "Messrs. Darton, Martin's publishers, in especial used to prefix the name [Peter Parley] to all sorts of children's books, without reference to their actual authorship."

Isaiah Thomas may be taken as representative of our Revolutionary period, even as the "New England Primer" may typify the chief literary product of our Colonial life. Peter Parley marks for us the war of 1812. It was after this that our country began to expand, that the South and the Southwest unfolded their possibilities, that the East began the Westward move that led to the craze of '49. The Indian, the scout, the cowboy, the Yankee trader have been the original contributions of America to juvenile literature. A close study will indicate that Cooper was the creator of this *genre* of story,—more painstaking, more effulgent, more detailed than the Indian story-writer of to-day, but none the less a permanent model. So, too, he will be found, in his accounts of the navy, in his records of common seamen, in his lives of naval officers, to be no mean, no inaccurate, no dry historian; in fact, Cooper, as one of our first naval critics, has yet to be accorded his proper estimate.

American history, American development being of a melodramatic character, it is natural that the opposite to Sunday-school literature should rapidly take root as soon as begun. A period of the ten-cent novel flourished about 1860, when the Beadle Brothers, who were finally to be merged into the publishing house of George Munro, began the publication of their series of cheap volumes—the sensationalism of Cooper raised to the nth power. To-day there are men who glow with remembered enthusiasm over Colonel Prentiss Ingraham and the detective stories of A. W. Aiken—whose record was often one a week—as they do over the name of Hemyng *alias* Jack Harkaway, or Mayne Reid, with his traditional profanity. Edward S. Ellis (b. 1840) was one of the young members of this group of writers. He became inoculated, but was forced, when the milder process came into vogue, to soften his high lights, and to accord with the times. What such early "wild cat" literature did, however, for present upholders of the "series" books, was to exemplify that, by a given pattern, a tale could be made to "go" to order. There was then, as there is now, a certain type of book, neither moral nor immoral, and not at all educational, but only momentarily diverting; written without motive, without definite object, but whose ground plan and mechanism were workable.

The increase of the public-school system was the chief opponent of the Sunday-school book, as it likewise, by its educational emphasis, fought against the dime-novel vogue. And with the inception of the public school on its present large scale we reach the immediate stage, the era of over-productivity, with its enormous average taste, with its public regard for readers in the libraries, for scholars in the class-rooms, for the poor in settlements, and for the emigrant on the high seas.

After an experience of five years in reviewing juvenile books of the past and in estimating the varied stories of the present, I do not think it sweeping to assert that while education has snatched the child's book from the moralist and taken away from writing a false standard of right doing, it has not, as yet, added any worthy attribute of itself. It has not taught the child to judge good literature from the bad; it has supplied, in a prescribed course, certain isolated books or stereotyped poems, with which the child is wearied in the class-room, and from which, once outside, the child turns with natural dread. I am judging solely from the standpoint of juvenile taste. And so, with the entrance of a new consideration—the children's reading-rooms—it may well be queried at the outset: What will this institution add to the creative force? How far will it seek to improve conditions? Will there be an increased demand for the good and for the best books? Will there be a more careful art manifested in the writing of stories? Will the gaps in the field be filled up? For an examination of the past and of the present tells me that children's literature, generally speaking, has yet to be conquered.

With these remarks in view, the table that follows may, on examination, bear some significance.

AMERICAN TABLE

NOAH WEBSTER. Ct. 1758–1843. Cf. Mavor in England. Author: New England Spelling Book; American Dictionary. Reference: Memoir by Goodrich (in Dictionary); Life by H. E. Scudder; Appleton.[45]

JEDIDIAH MORSE. Ct. 1761–1826. Congregational minister; wrote first school text-books of any importance in America. His son was S. F. B. Morse. Author: Geography Made Easy, etc. He is called the "Father of American Geography." Reference: Life by Sprague; Appleton.

THOMAS HOPKINS GALLAUDET. Ct. 1787–1851. Minister. Educator of deaf mutes; in this work assisted by wife, Sophia Fowler (1798–1877), and two sons. Author: The Child's Book of the Soul; The Youth's Book of Natural Theology; Bible Stories for the Young. Reference: Life by Humphrey; Tribute to T. H. G. by Henry Barnard (Hartford, Conn., 1852); Appleton.

ELIZA LESLIE. Pa. 1787–1857. Wrote cook books, girls' books, and juvenile tales for *The Pearl and The Violet*, which she edited annually. She also edited *The Gift*. One of her brothers, a well-known artist. Author: The Young Americans; Stories for Adelaide; Stories for Helen; The Behaviour Book. The Wonderful Traveller consisted of altered versions of tales from Münchausen, Gulliver, etc. Reference: Appleton.

MRS. SARAH JOSEPHA (BUELL) HALE. N. H. 1788–1879. It was through her efforts that Thanksgiving became an American national observance. Her son, Horatio, was an author. Author: The famous "Mary had a little lamb." Edited *Lady's Book* for forty years from 1837. Reference: Appleton.

CATHERINE MARIA SEDGWICK. Mass. 1789–1867. Author: The Boy of Mount Rhigi, a tale of inspired goodness; Beatitudes and Pleasant Sundays; The Poor Rich Man and the Rich Poor Man; A Love Token for Children; Morality of Manners; Lessons without Books. Reference: Hart's Female Prose Writers of America; Life and Letters, ed. Mary E. Dewey; Appleton.

MRS. SUSAN (RIDLEY) SEDGWICK. Mass. 1789–1867. Author: Walter Thornley; Morals of Pleasure; The Young Emigrants. Reference: Appleton.

MRS. LYDIA HOWARD (HUNTLEY) SIGOURNEY. Ct. 1791–1865. Author: Letters to Young Ladies; Poetry for Children; Tales and Essays for Children. Reference: Griswold's Female Poets; Hart's Female Prose Writers; Life and Letters; Parton's Eminent Women; Appleton.

MRS. CAROLINE (HOWARD) GILMAN. Mass. 1794–1888. Took great pride in her children's books. Began writing in *Southern Rosebud* (Charleston), afterward called *Southern Rose* (1832–1839). This magazine has been credited as the first juvenile weekly in the United States. Her daughter, Caroline H. (b. S. C. 1823), also wrote for the young. Author: Oracles for Youth; Mrs. Gilman's Gift Book. Reference: Autobiographical sketch in Hart's Female Prose Writers; Recollections; Appleton.

MRS. LOUISA C. (HUGGINS) TUTHILL. Ct. 1798–1897. Wrote moral tales; with others prepared Juvenile Library for Boys and Girls; her daughter, Cornelia (T.) Pierson (1820–1870), wrote Our Little Comfort; When Are We Happiest? Author: I will be a Gentleman; I will be a Lady; I will be a Sailor; Onward, Right Onward. Edited the Young Ladies Reader (New Haven, 1840). Reference: Hart; Appleton.

JOHN TODD. Vt. 1800–1873. Invented Index Rerum. Author: Religious works, mainly for young people; also educational works. Reference: Life; *Harper's Magazine*, Feb., 1876.

LYDIA MARIA CHILD. Mass. 1802–1880. Foremost in the ranks of anti-slavery; influenced by Garrison. In 1826, founded the *Juvenile Miscellany*, forerunner of Harper's *Young People*. Author: Flowers for Children (graded). Reference: Hart; Nat. Cyclo. Am. Biog.

MARIA J. MCINTOSH. Ga. 1803–1878. Quiet and domestic tone to her books. Author: Series known as the Aunt Kitty Tales, the first one being Blind Alice, published in 1841. Reference: Hart.

DR. HARVEY NEWCOMB. Mass. 1803–1866. Congregational clergyman. Wrote moral and religious books for young. Author: How to be a Man; How to be a Lady; Young Ladies' Guide. Reference: Appleton.

REV. JACOB ABBOTT. Me. 1803–1879. Divinity school; Professor at Amherst; Congregationalist. Travelled extensively. Author: Rollo books (28 vols.); Lucy books (6 vols.); Jonas books (6 vols.); Franconia books (10 vols.); histories with brother (*vide* p. 160). Reference: A Neglected N. E. Author (*N. E. Mag.*, n. s. 30:471); Writings (*Lit. and Theol. R.*, 3:83); (*Chr. Exam.*, 18:133; 21:306); Appleton.

REV. ABIJAH RICHARDSON BAKER. Mass. 1805–1876. Congregationalist. Graduate of Amherst; a teacher. With his wife, Mrs. H. N. W. Baker, edited *The Mother's Assistant* and *The Happy Home*. Author: School History of the U. S.; Westminster Shorter Catechism—Graduated Question Book. Reference: Appleton.

J. S. C. ABBOTT. Me. 1805–1877. Brother of Jacob Abbott. Congregational minister. Author: The Mother at Home; histories with brother. Reference: *Cong. Q.*, 20:1; Appleton.

SARAH TOWNE (SMITH) MARTYN. 1805–1879. Wife of a minister. Wrote Sunday-school books and semi-historical stories. Published through American Tract Society. Established *Ladies' Wreath*, and edited it, 1846–1851. Author: Huguenots of France; Lady Alice Lisle. Reference: Appleton.

MRS. ELIZABETH OAKES (PRINCE) SMITH. Me. 1806–1893. One of the first women lecturers in America. Moved later to South Carolina. By her book, The Newsboy, public attention was drawn to that class of child. Supervised, *circa* 1840, annual issuance of the *Mayflower* (Boston). Author: The Sinless Child; Stories for Children; Hints on Dress and Beauty. Reference: Hart; Nat. Cyclo. Am. Biog.

MARY STANLEY BUNCE (PALMER) (DANA) SHINDLER. S. C. 1810–1883. Wife of a clergyman, Episcopal. Author: Charles Morton; or, The Young Patriot; The Young Sailor. Reference: Appleton.

HARRIET BEECHER STOWE. Ct. 1811–1896. Author: Dred; Uncle Tom's Cabin. Reference: Life work of,—McCray; E. F. Parker in Parton's Eminent Women; Life compiled from letters and journals by C. E. Stowe; Life and Letters, ed. Annie Fields.

ELIJAH KELLOGG. Me. 1813-. Congregational minister. Famed for "The Address of Spartacus to the Gladiators." Author: Elm Island series; Forest Glen series; Good Old Times series; Pleasant Cove series. Reference: Bibliog. Me.; Appleton.

MARY ELIZABETH LEE. S. C. 1813–1849. Not a distinctive juvenile writer, but contributed many juvenile tales to *The Rosebud*. (*Vide* Gilman.) Reference: Hart.

REV. ZACHARIAH ATWELL MUDGE. Mass. 1813–1888. Methodist-Episcopal minister; teacher. Fiction for Sunday-schools. Author: Arctic Heroes; Fur Clad Adventurers. Reference: Appleton.

MRS. HARRIET V. CHENEY. Mass. *Circa* 1815. Daughter of Hannah Foster, an early American novelist. Her sister, Mrs. Cushing, wrote Esther, a dramatic poem, and "works" for the young. Author: A Peep at the Pilgrims; The Sunday-school; or, Village Sketches. Reference: Appleton.

MRS. HARRIETTE NEWELL (WOODS) BAKER. Mass. 1815–1893. Pseud. Madeline Leslie. Wife of Rev. A. R. B. Author: About two hundred moral tales, among them Tim, the Scissors Grinder. Reference: Appleton.

LYDIA ANN EMERSON (PORTER). Mass. 1816-. Second cousin of Ralph Waldo Emerson. Contributed mostly to the Sunday-school type of book. Author: Uncle Jerry's Letters to Young Mothers; The Lost Will. Reference: Appleton.

CATHERINE MARIA TROWBRIDGE. Ct. 1818-. Author: Christian Heroism; Victory at Last; Will and Will Not; Snares and Safeguards.

SUSAN WARNER. N. Y. 1818–1885. Pseud. Elizabeth Wetherell. Books noted for strained religious sentimentality. With her, the school of Hannah More came to an end. Author: The Wide, Wide World (1851); Queechy (1852); Say and Seal (in collaboration with her sister). Reference: Appleton.

REV. WILLIAM MAKEPEACE THAYER. Mass. 1820–1898. Congregational minister; member of legislature. Author: Youth's History of the Rebellion; The Bobbin Boy; The Pioneer Boy; The Printer Boy; Men Who Win; Women Who Win. Edited *The Home Monthly* and *The Mother's Assistant*. Reference: Appleton.

WILLIAM TAYLOR ADAMS. Mass. 1822–1897. Pseud. Oliver Optic. In early life ed. *Student and School-Mate*. In 1881, ed. *Our Little Ones*. Then ed. *Oliver Optic's Magazine*. Author: About one hundred volumes; first one published 1853, Hatchie, the Guardian Slave. Reference: Appleton.

CHARLES CARLETON COFFIN. N. H. 1823–1896. Self-educated. Varied career as a war correspondent during the Civil War. Author: The Boys of '76. Reference: Life by Griffis; Appleton.

WILLIAM HENRY THOMAS. 1824–1895. Belonged to the school of dime novelists. Boys in the 60's eagerly devoured the Beadle and (later) Munro books. Author: The Belle of Australia; Ocean Rover; A Whaleman's Adventure. Reference: Appleton.

MRS. ALICE (BRADLEY) (NEAL) HAVEN. N. Y. 1828–1863. Pseud. Alice G. Lee. Wrote for Sunday-schools. Author: No such Word as Fail; Contentment Better Than Wealth. Reference: Memoir in *Harper's Magazine*, Oct., 1863; Appleton.

JANE ANDREWS. Mass. 1833–1887. Author: Seven Little Sisters who live on the Round Ball that Floats in the Air; The Stories Mother Nature Told.

CHARLES A. FOSDICK. N. Y. 1842-. Pseud. Harry Castlemon. Went through the Civil War. Author: Gunboat series; Rocky Mountains series; Roughing It series; Frank series; Archie series.

MRS. ANNIE M. MITCHELL. Mass. 1847-. Religious books for children. Author: Martha's Gift; Freed Boy in Alabama.

MRS. MARY L. CLARK. Fairford, Me. 1831-. Religious juveniles. Author: The Mayflower series; Daisy's Mission.

MRS. CAROLINE E. DAVIS. Northwood, N. H. 1831-. Sunday-school tales, about fifty or more. Author: No Cross, No Crown; Little Conqueror Series; Miss Wealthy's Hope; That Boy; Child's Bible Stories. Reference: Appleton.

SARA H. BROWNE. Author: Book for the Eldest Daughter (1849).

MARIA J. BROWNE. Author: The Youth's Sketch Book (1850). Reference for both: Hart (Bibl.).

III. THE PRESENT SITUATION.

The essential difference between the past and the present is not so much a difference, after all; in both instances the same mistaken emphasis is placed upon two separate phases of the child's make-up. The moral tale took no cognisance of those spiritual laws which are above teaching, which act of themselves; it did not recognise the existence of the child's personality. But when the impetus toward the study, scientific and intensive, of adolescence was begun, the teacher lost sight of the free will by which that growth advanced; anxious to prove the child's development to be but a series of stages marked by educational gradings, he reserved no place for the self-development through which the personality finds expression. In both cases an unconscious injustice was done juvenile nature. The moral questioning warped the spirit, the educational questioning chokes the imagination and fancy, starving the spirit altogether. How many will agree with Emerson's assertion that "what we do not call education is more precious than that which we call so"? The pessimist who challenges children's books for children has reasons to doubt, after all.

Time changes not, 'tis we who change in time. Emerson speaks in terms of evolution; by this very change from generation to generation, the vitality of a book is tested. Again, in terms of our mentality, Emerson says that when a thought of Plato becomes a thought to us, Time is no more. Truth is thus an annihilator of the fleeting moment. The survival of the fittest means the falling away of the mediocre. The Sunday-school book was no permanent type; its content was no classic expression. It filled a timely demand—that was its excuse for being. Once this demand became modified, the book's service was at an end; hence Mr. Welsh's indication of the decline of the Sunday-school story through secularisation,—from sectarianism to broad religious principles, thence to "example rather than direct teaching."[46]

We still have the religious tract and the church story-paper; yet the books of advice deal with the social and ethical spirit, rather than with the denominational stricture. "The less a man thinks or knows about his virtues, the better we like him," wrote Emerson, while Stevenson, in his "Lay Sermons," placed the stress thus: "It is the business of life to make excuses for others but not for ourselves."

To-morrow new topics may be introduced into our juvenile literature, but change takes longer than a day to become apparent. The student who attempts to reach any scientific estimate of the present trend will be disappointed; the mass is too conglomerate, and there are too many authors writing children's books for money rather than for children. I have followed the course as carefully as I could, noting the slight alterations in concepts to accord with the varying conditions. But there is no principle that can be deduced, other than the educational one. The changes are confined to points of external interest, not of spiritual or mental significance. For instance, there was a time when girls' literature and boys' literature were more clearly differentiated, one from the other; their near approach has been due to a common interest in outdoor exercises. Again, things practical, things literal have crowded out the benignant figure of Santa Claus; and in the stead, the comic supplement of the Sunday newspaper furnishes pictures that well-nigh stifle the true domain once occupied by "Mother Goose."

What would a parent do, asked suddenly to deal with a promiscuous collection of juvenile books? Would she unerringly reach forth for the volume most likely to please her son's or her daughter's taste? If she were to claim little difference between the one college story she had read, and the several hundred she had not read, she would not be far from wrong. But we cannot tell how deep an impression the present activity among writers for children will have on the future. Our temptation is to make the general statement that the energy is a surface one, that no great writing is being done for children because it has become an accessory rather than an end in itself. Education saved us from the moral pose; it must not deny us the realm of imagination and fancy.

FOOTNOTES

[41] In education, the influence of Froebel, in direct descent from Rousseau, is to be considered.

[42] D. N. B.—Dictionary of National Biography.

[43] The student who desires to investigate the history of American schoolbooks will find much valuable material in the Watkinson Library of Hartford, Conn., to which institution Dr. Henry Barnard's entire collection of school-

books was left. *Vide* Bibliotheca Americana, Catalogue of American Publications, including reprints and original works, from 1820 to 1852, inclusive, together with a list of periodicals published in the United States, compiled and arranged by Orville A. Roorbach, N. Y., Oct., 1852. Includes Supplement to 1849 ed., published in 1850.

Vide also Early English School-books. Educational Library, South Kensington Museum.

[44] *Vide* Recollections of a Life-time; or, Men and Things I have Seen: in a series of familiar Letters to a Friend. Historical, Biographical, Anecdotal, and Descriptive. S. G. Goodrich. (2 vols.) New York, 1857. [Contains a valuable list of the real Parley books; also the names of the spurious Parleys. The volumes describe many small characteristics of American life during the early years of the nineteenth century.]

[45] Cyclopædia.

[46] Mr. Welsh states that between 1706–1718, 550 books were published in America, of which 84 were *not* religious, and of these 84, 49 were almanacs!

V.
THE LIBRARY AND THE BOOK

THE LAND OF STORY-BOOKS

At evening when the lamp is lit,
Around the fire my parents sit;
They sit at home and talk and sing,
And do not play at anything.
Now, with my little gun, I crawl
All in the dark along the wall,
And follow round the forest track
Away behind the sofa back.
There, in the night, where none can spy,
All in my hunter's camp I lie,
And play at books that I have read
Till it is time to go to bed.
These are the hills, these are the woods,
These are my starry solitudes;
And there the river by whose brink
The roaring lions come to drink.
I see the others far away
As if in firelit camp they lay,
And I, like to an Indian scout,
Around their party prowled about.
So, when my nurse comes in for me,
Home I return across the sea,
And go to bed with backward looks
At my dear land of Story-books.

—Robert Louis Stevenson, in
"A Child's Garden of Verses."

I. Children's Books: Their Classification; Their Characteristics.

There is nothing more variegated in its colour than a large assemblage of children's books; the cover-designers revel in their rainbow conceits, sprinkling gold across the cloth as generously as fairies scatter star-dust; the artists fill their brushes with delicate tints of red and blue and orange, and sketch the progress of a story in spiral traceries of imagination. The mechanical perfection of book-making is genuinely pleasing; the form, like that of the glass-blown vase with its slender outlines, is fitted for the worthiest content. The excellence of binding, the distinctness of type, the spirit of the drawing—these points strike our senses, these are the subterfuges of the publishing trade, these the artistic features that hide the shallowness beneath. You may arrange your blue books together, and your red, your brown, your white or green in rows; you may mix them all up again, and marshal them in regiments of equal sizes; the persistent query stares you in the face,—the stinging fact of ignorance—what of the story you are about to buy?

In the public library, the shelves are empty; you are told, as the librarian, to fill them. Not for yourself alone is the choice to be made, or even for your own children, whom you are supposed to know; but for every one who wishes to read. You have little right to assume much homogeneity of taste or desire among young folks; you must balance your dreams with facts, your ideals with human accomplishment. We are all as grains of sand in the general scheme of the universe; we are all supposed to have equal chances before the law; but what we are is the measure of what we read. You are the custodian of a public trust, not of your private book-case. A row of children—the poor by the side of the rich, the newsboy by the side of the patrician—you are to supply them every one. Have you then the privilege of assuming an autocratic policy of exclusion? Can you say to yourself, The newsboy must read Homer!—and refrain from buying him his penny-dreadful?

Each man's standard of excellence differs from his neighbour's. Matthew Arnold's idea of the best ignored your opinion and mine. The world has put a face value on certain books; they live because the universal in them and the universal in us is constant and persistent. And though we each stand upon a different pivot of existence, though the wind blows with less fury around you than around me, on calm nights we may each see the same star, however different the angle of vision.

So, are you not here furnished a starting-point in your purchases? Where you are concerned with children, your opportunity is richer by far than you first imagined. They have no preconceived notions; they stand in a general mystery of dawning experience; they know not how or why; all truth is a fable before them. Common things are apparelled in celestial light; nature is governed by omnipotence; creation is the first meeting with Aladdin's lamp. The common law of growth tells us this; our knowledge of men is carved from such general mystery; our method of gaining this experience is higher than we wot of; the father is judged in terms of King Arthur before he is reckoned with as a man.

Therefore, it is your bounden duty to satisfy these several stages. You must have pictures for the little ones that will cater to a familiarity with common things, and will satisfy a tendency in them to make all nature animate.[47] You must find an artist capable of seeing the significance, the humour of the dish running after the spoon. There must be picture-books that will treat of these things with all the purity they deserve; high-mindedness is an essential part of elemental fun. The nursery claims a part in your plan. Place, then, first upon your list, the best picture-books and jingles. Let true art supplant the comic supplement sheet.

We will banish the use of baffling terms in speaking of the classes of juvenile books. Our Fiction will become Stories; our Myths and Folk-lore and Fables simply Fairy Tales and Legends. Our arrangement now assumes a definite perspective, from the limitless past to ourselves as the fixed point. Our standard is one of interest; we will apply the test of excellence, not to books generally, but to each channel in which individual interest has a right to seek its own development. By a psychological consideration, we are able to hitch our wagon to a star, to span the distance separating the Present and the Past, the Real and the Ideal. Myth flows imperceptibly into legend; and, with all the massive proportions of the heroic, legend enters and becomes part of history. And history is vitalised only when we present it to children in the form of biography. Is it not Carlyle who defines history as the biography of great men?

Thus, we add still more to the positive factors in our book selecting. We will not disguise for the child the true character of a volume by a nomenclature which is indefinite. Better the terms "How We Are Governed" than "Civics"; and "How to Make Things" than "Manual Training." We will satisfy all tastes by the best to be had, and that rule shall be proverbial. The boy, deprived of his dime novel,[48] must be given something just as daring, just as redolent with sensationalism; but we will transfer his den of thieves from the areaway to the broad green forest, and his profession of robbery shall grow into outlawry; his Jesse James become Robin Hood. Some of the best literature contains the quality of sensationalism; it is the form that the dime novel has taken, and the cheap exploitation of filthy detail, that have obscured many of the most beneficial elements in melodrama. The Adventures of Ulysses, the Twelve Labours of Hercules, Daniel in the Lion's Den, Jonathan and David—the green lights are not far away.

Have you ever watched the breathlessness of a messenger boy with his "Ragged Dick Series"; the intent, eager faces in the gallery of the theatre during a melodrama? Nine times out of ten, morals are not being perverted; crime is not being glorified, but severely punished; chivalry is acting in shirt-sleeves; the good is winning its just deserts in a large way, and the boy glows. Not that I would have our libraries circulate "Ragged Dick," but there is more to remember in such stimulation, there is more *effect* than will ever be drawn from the conventional tale with its customary noble and ignoble heroes. The amount of inane fiction concocted for children is pernicious.

Literature has been made cold to the child, yet there is nothing warmer than a classic, when properly handled. Each man lives in his own age; we are creatures of timeliness, but we see the clearer for being at times on the mountain peak. The traveller from an antique land is part of our experience quite as much as the man around the corner. What I contend is that the attraction, the appeal of a story depends largely on the telling. With a broad sweep of right emotion, we must be taught to soar, and there must be no penalty of arrest for wishing to o'erleap the false horizon of a city skyline. The tenement boy is a dreamer, even though he perforce must lay his cheek against the rough brick of an air-shaft and squint up at the stars. The democracy of a public library system affords him equal opportunities with Keats—even though he may not have the same capacity for enjoyment—to look into Chapman's Homer; he is entitled to all that vast experience, that same "hoard of goodly states and kingdoms." But if his author is not deep-browed, if he, too, is not given the same pure serenity of view, if his Chapman does not speak out loud and bold, he will feel himself defrauded of the vitalising meaning of literature, he will have missed being

... like some watcher of the skies

When a new planet swims into his ken.

This, therefore, should make you determine to cry against mediocrity; to purchase for those empty shelves the best of a class, the best of an edition, and the most authentic of texts.

Lady Eastlake once wrote: "The real secret of a child's book consists not merely in its being less dry and less difficult, but more rich in interest, more true to nature, more exquisite in art, more abundant in every quality that replies to childhood's keener and fresher perceptions. Such being the case, the best of juvenile reading will be found in libraries belonging to their elders, while the best juvenile writing will not fail to delight those who are no longer children. 'Robinson Crusoe,' the standing favourite of above a century, was not originally written for children; and Sir Walter Scott's 'Tales of a Grandfather,' addressed solely to them, are the pleasure and profit of every age, from childhood upward. Our little friends tear Pope's 'Odyssey' from mamma's hands, while she takes up their 'Agathos'[49] with an admiration which no child's can exceed."

The opinion here quoted somewhat overstates the real case. The experienced librarian of to-day could tell a different tale from the loan desk; it is the average young person she must have in mind, and the average understanding. But this understanding is not commensurate with the reading ability of the child; it is much above it, and this fact also should be considered an asset for the librarian to work with. Despite the theories regarding how a story should be told to a seven-year-old reader, and to one twelve years old, the volumes do not very consistently adapt themselves to such a classification. The buyer must say: Is it to be read *by* the child? Consider his schooling. Is it to be read *to* the child? Consider his understanding.

Let us not subject ourselves to the criticism that our ideals will not work. If they are impractical, they are useless and must be amended. It is recognised that something more is wanted than the "masterpiece," so guardedly extolled by Mr. Everett T. Tomlinson,[50] a popular author of boys' books. He separates the boy and the classic by a wide gulf of adolescent requirements; he pleads for something in addition to bone and tendon; he believes the boy demands material to fit his mental estate, which is not equipped for "ready response" to adult literature. In other words, the juvenile book of to-day, which is well typified by his own stories, is to supplement and not to supplant the "masterpiece."

The situation is a rather delicate and uncertain one; it would be well, as Mr. Tomlinson suggests, if the results, as he thinks, were actually the case. But does the girl, who reads her "series" trilogy, slip from Dinsmore into Dickens; or does the boy, with his Henty books filling shelf after shelf, graduate therefrom into Scott? The theory does not work, and, even if it did, an immense amount of energy is going to waste somewhere. Miss Hewins, from her extensive experience as a worker in the Hartford Public Library, has outlined what you can get from a Henty book [Wisconsin Library Bulletin. Madison, Sept.-Oct., 1906. Vol. 2, No. 5.]; her plan is most interesting, and, were there readers possessing the zeal necessary to make such literature permanently serviceable, we could actually view knowledge growing from more to more. The summary is as follows:

"If a boy reads nothing but Henty for a year or so, he is not likely to care for the great historical novels of the world later, but if he uses him under guidance, reading after each one of his books a better story of the same period, if he look up places on a map, unfamiliar words and references in a dictionary or cyclopædia, and if he reads a life of one of the real characters in every book, he is well on his way to an intelligent interest in general history."

But would it not be just as well to centre this concentration directly on Scott? The librarian will doubtless claim that the boy turns more readily to the one than to the other, and I believe that this is largely due to the over-emphasis of Scott as a standard author, and of Henty as a popular writer for boys. Scott has never been issued in form to catch the young reader's eye. Given as many illustrations as Henty, relegating the preface to the appendix, or omitting it altogether, and the author of "Waverley" would be found to have lost none of his grip. You will receive from any librarian the unfailing statement that one of the most constant ambitions is to reduce the proportion of fiction in circulation, and, in that proportion, to preserve what is of true worth in place of the mediocre average of the modern story-books.

Mr. Tomlinson's analysis of the qualities in a child's book may be indicated by seven divisions:

a.   There must be a story.

b.   There must be vigorous action with little contemplation. "Analysis and introspection are words outside of his [the child's] vocabulary," says Mr. Tomlinson.

c.   Fancy is more to be sought for than pure imagination.

d.   The writer must regard the moral character of boys: a lack of mercy, a strict sense of justice; he must regard their faith which is credulity; their sentiment of reverence; their power of being convinced.

e.   The writer must likewise consider the differences between the sexes in the point of moral faculties, even though in many respects they are the same. For girls have tender consciences, though not so tenacious; they are quick to promise, and as quick to forget; they are easily stirred to pity, their sympathy easily appealed to. Bringing it down to an animalistic basis, Mr. Tomlinson believes that though the ancestral cruelty in girls is not so evident as in boys, when it does flash forth it is sharper in every way. "To both, right and wrong are absolute, not relative terms, and a youthful misanthrope is as much of an anomaly as a youthful grandfather."

f.   The sentiments must be directed in channels of usefulness and power, hence the story of patriotism, the situation of courage, the incident of tenderness.

g.   Since the faculties in action are receptive, rather than perceptive, since the memory is keen to hold, the writer must bear this psychological status in mind.

In fine, recognising that even in his play the boy takes things seriously, and believing that the juvenile intellect "seeks the reasonable more than the process of reasoning," Mr. Tomlinson shapes a dicta of criticism, a standard by which the child's book may be recognised in terms of vital characteristics. Apply them to recent juvenile books, if you will, and you will find the majority wanting. But will not the classics meet these requirements? Are we to relegate the best we have to the back shelves, and buy nothing that smacks of good style? Instead of putting tight bands of expectancy about our minds, and of making us bow down before a throne of iced classics, let the librarian treat the "Iliad" genially, let her represent "Siegfried" with the broad heavens above him. The classics have *yielding* power.

It is characteristic of every age that a discontent is always manifest with the conditions as they exist at the time. As early as 1844, the child's book, *per se*, was brought under rigourous scrutiny by an unnamed critic in the *Quarterly Review*, and what was said then applies equally as well to the state of affairs to-day. But this very entertaining writer, talking in terms of judgment founded upon a keen understanding of what such a book should be, attempts a list of juvenile books which bears all the ear-marks of his age; he finds it necessary to select from the immediate supply; he knows that there is the author of his own era whom he cannot discard. We have a lurking suspicion that, with his canons of criticism, he would have altered his list, could he have looked in perspective. But there was very little range in children's books of that day; the species was just becoming accentuated, and his element of *timeliness* had to be regarded. Therefore, while we are pleading with the librarian for a high choice in the selection of books, we know that were the *timely* volume omitted, simply on the basis that it did not conform with one's idea of the best, the library would become fixed, like a dead language. The *Quarterly* article was written at a time when the secularisation of juvenile literature was just beginning to take place; the moral and the educational factors were looking askance, the one at the other, both claiming the boy and girl for instruction, but each from a different basis. Our author pleads for the healthy, normal reader, in whom "still-born" knowledge—mere lifeless acquisition—were a curse indeed! He cries out against the educational catechism, as he does against the moral one. His discriminating thesis advances in threefold manner, for he writes:

"Those who insist on keeping the sense of enjoyment rigidly back, till that of comprehension has been forcibly urged forward—who stipulate that the one shall not be indulged till the other be appeased—are in reality but retarding what they most affect to promote."

And again:

"Children have no sooner begun to enjoy than they are called upon to reflect; they have no sooner begun to forget that there exists in the world such a little being as themselves than they are pulled back to remember, not only what they are, but what they will one day infallibly become."

And still again:

"Children seem to possess an inherent conviction that when the hole is big enough for the cat, no smaller one at the side is needed for the kitten. They do not really care for 'Glimpses' of this, or 'Gleanings' of that, or 'Footsteps' to the other—they would rather stretch and pull...."

From a desert of dust-covered magazines, this comes to us like a hidden spring bubbling with energy which no outer crust of years can quell.[51] Then as now, they had the pernicious school-book—instance Peter Parley;[52] then as now, they had the flippant tale. Our unknown author recommended "Puss in Boots," with designs by Otto Specker, as the beau ideal of nursery books, and the Grimm Tales with Cruikshank's illustrations; he recognised the admirable qualities in the verses by the Taylor sisters. Miss Edgeworth, Miss Tytler, Mrs. Barbauld, Mrs. Hofland, Mary Howitt (although some of her books are questioned), Catherine Sinclair, Mrs. Marcet, and a host of others, now dead to the circulating shelves, received their quota of commendation. The list is a curious example of existing circumstances; it illustrates the futility of crystallising the library system; it demonstrates that the library, as an institution, must reflect the aspirations of its age, not overreaching its full capacity of usefulness and of average excellence.

II. THE LIBRARY, THE SCHOOL, THE HOME: A PLEA FOR CULTURE.

"Criticism," says Matthew Arnold, "must maintain its independence of the practical spirit and its aims. Even with well-meant efforts of the practical spirit it must express dissatisfaction, if in the sphere of the ideal they seem impoverishing and limiting." Still, not for a moment are we able to lose sight of the active working conditions of the library. Speculation as to the functions of such an institution in a community may lead to the formulation of certain ideals which are to guide the practical machinery in the future. But, on the instant, there is the urgent necessity of supply and demand; the theorist must cope with the actual reader calling for a book.

It is, however, only proper to expect that human activity be directed, not along the lines of least resistance, but along the lines of best results. This infers that the library, as an institution, fully recognises that it has a function to perform in society, and that it will strive, in its several capacities, so to unify its activities that it will become a force as well as a convenience.

Through pleasure, we would train the child to future usefulness; physically we would let him find expression for all his surplus energy; but as a reader, we would so far guide him that none of his mental energy will go to waste. Intellectually, a boy or a girl should not be given what one library called "leisure hour reading"; a book should not mean, for either, a vehicle for frittering the time away, but their training should lead to the finding of "tongues in trees, books in the running brooks, sermons in stones, and good in everything."

An essential purpose is a most important element in the future history of children's rooms, and at the present initial stage it were unwise to criticise the methods by which the library is trying to state this purpose in definite terms. But whether we regard its activity in the direction of the home, the school, the settlement, or the city at large, we may safely claim that its main duty in all directions is to supply the best books to be had on any stated line. And herein we discover the connection that ought to exist between our schools as educational, and our libraries as cultural centres. In Buffalo, Mr. Melvil Dewey, during an address given to teachers, said:

"By law, the children are put under your influence in their earlier years, when, if ever, they can be taught to love good books so well that in all their lives thereafter they will seize on every opportunity to read them. If the librarians, with their wing of the educational army, can select and catalogue and provide free of cost the best on every subject, the schoolmen, with their wing and with their immensely larger resources both of money and men—and still better, of devoted women—must send out from the schools, year by year, boys and girls who will be lifelong patrons of the public library, and will, in due time, help to send their own children along the paths which have proved for them so profitable and pleasant; ... but its great work should be the partial recognition that education is no longer for youth and for a limited course, in a school to which they give most of their time, but that it is really a matter for adults as well as youth, for life and not for the course, to be carried on at home as well as in the schools, and to be taken up in the hours or minutes of leisure, as the proper accompaniment of their regular business or labour. This means that education must be carried on by means of reading, and that, if the librarians are to furnish the books and give all necessary help in their proper field, the schools must furnish the readers."

It is, therefore, the supreme function of a supervisor of school libraries to reconcile culture with knowledge-getting—taste and desire with mental training—quite as much as it is his official duty to furnish supplementary books for the class-rooms. In fact, the former should become his chief business, for in the other capacity he slightly encroaches upon, rather than aids—duplicates in expense, rather than enforces by supplying a need—the work being done by the neighbourhood library.

Between the school and the library there should thus be a reciprocal interchange of courtesies, the sum total of which tends toward culture.[53] For the child is the potential man, and in our reading, despite the opportunities for education, we are not made to understand, at the early age when habits are most readily formed, the real import of the sustaining power of art.

The reading of novels is a delightful recreation; it is not the reading which should be questioned; it is the power to stop. Periods of rest are a psychological necessity, but it is the power of returning from the side issue to the life issue, which, in so many cases, is the missing element. The literature that does nothing more than amuse is not the literature which, in future days, one is to fall back on as a maintaining force. Browning cries out:

I count life just a stuff

To try the soul's strength on, educe the man.

The man of culture is something more than an upstart; his is a slow but a steady growth; the smallest star that burns into the night is one whose rays have taken years to reach the earth. Out of the varied but unified elements, the personality evolves its view of life; it may not necessarily be a life among books; Shakespeare the man and Shakespeare the poet are contradictions. The sustaining force in literature is no protector in the sense that it shields us from some impending danger. It settles behind us, pushes us, heart and soul, with a burning resolution, through the darkest night. The cultured man finds himself clinging to the sunnier side of doubt, not because Tennyson advises it, but because it has become part of his philosophy; he falls back upon a part of himself developed by literature.

Our neighbour is but a composite picture of numberless developments, all working toward a definite goal. We call him the cultured man. Our neighbour is one who tries to show us as many pictures of himself, working in different directions, as he thinks will clothe him in a mist of thought. We call him the dilettante. Dilettanteism does not sustain; we either have to be perfectly honest with ourselves, or else be discovered by others in the end.

The habit of association with good books is, therefore, one which our school systems need to inculcate. The supervisor of class-room libraries should strive to supplement the text-book with something that is not a text-book; the outlines of history should be strengthened by *bona fide* biography instead of by the hybrid type of fiction. A committee in Germany, after working some years over the recommendations of books for children, finally printed a list of 637 volumes—calling attention to a weakness in travel, popular science, and biography. This condition is as true in England and America; and one of the causes for the deficiency may be accounted for by the substitution of the text-book style for the dignified narrative. The writer of juvenile books, other than fiction, has not realised, up to the present time, that the direct treatment is capable of being understood by young people.

Conscious of this weakness, the librarian in time will banish from the circulating shelves the text-book, *per se*; and the school child should be prepared to meet the change. If he is given instruction in the uses of a dictionary,[54] and of a card catalogue; if he is trained by degrees to hunt up references—he should as well be familiarized with the transition from text-book to authority, from selection to source, from part to whole. From the mere usefulness of books he should be taught the attractive power of books. This, it would seem, is one of the fundamental relations existing between the library and the school.

With the increase of facilities, with the specialised consideration paid to children's reading by librarian and by teacher, there arises the factor of the parent in connection with the two. What part, in the general plan, does the home occupy? It furnishes the scholar; it furnishes the reader. In private instruction, it may dictate what shall be taught to the boy or girl; in public instruction, the individual becomes part of the system. The home may purchase books for the particular taste of this child or of that, but the public library must attend to *all* demands. Because of its democratic mission, it partially discourages the private ownership of books by the average person. Therefore, in most essentials, the State furnishes the means of instruction and indicates what that instruction shall be in its elementary stages; the State likewise supports the library, a repository where the regulation and censorship are minimised as far as the reader is concerned.

Let us acknowledge the peculiar social and economic conditions that conduce to deprive the home of the means or of the time to give to the proper training of children: the crowded tenement, the isolated mountain cabin are alike in this denial. But the school and the library are counteracting the deficiency. The mental condition in the tenement is more in a state of ferment than in the mountains; the second generation of the ignorant emigrant in New York or Chicago or Cleveland or Pittsburg is far more fortunate than the new generation peopling our Blue Ridge Mountains in Virginia. Yet the school and the library are penetrating the dense maze—they are defying isolation, and we will doubtless discover, before long, that the stagnation throughout the Tennessee ranges, and bordering the northern line of the Shenandoah Valley, has beneath it a great potential future of intellectual development. Until the social settlement passes through its experimental stage,—perhaps its very existence is dependent upon its experimental character—it were not safe to speculate on how largely it will aid in making the home so far independent of consuming necessity that it will respect the refinements of life, and will recognise that, in so doing, each individual raises his own self-respect. Should the settlement accomplish this, however little, it will justify its existence.

The home, none the less, remains a factor, and its responsibility is none the less urgent. The story hour is one of its legacies from the past, and through it, the parent should cater wisely to a child's desire for a tale. If the library is also adopting the same means, this in no way should relieve the parent of the prerogative; it should only afford her an opportunity of improving upon her own idea as to how a story should be told. Home influence should direct this juvenile desire, this individual taste; for no one has the close knowledge of a boy or girl possessed by the father or mother.

The habit of good reading, mentioned before, should be the joint product of the library, the school, and the home. Yet, in many instances, the library card of the child is of small consideration to the parent. This is more likely due to indifference than to an absolute confidence in the library's effort to bring juvenile readers in contact with the best books. The woman's club that will study the problem of children's reading, as sedulously as it analyses the pathologic significance of Ibsen's heroines, will be rendering a service to the library, as well as fitting its members to pass some judgment on the publisher's yearly output of juvenile books.

III. Book-lists and Book-selecting.

"Shall we permit our children," wrote Plato in the "Republic," "without scruple to hear any fables composed by any authors indifferently, and so to receive into their minds opinions generally the reverse of those which, when they are grown to manhood, we shall think they ought to entertain?" To a negative reply from Adeimantus, Glaucon's brother, Plato continued: "Then apparently our first duty will be to exercise a superintendence over the authors of fables, selecting their good productions, and rejecting the bad. And the selected fables we shall advise our nurses and mothers to repeat to their children, that they may thus mould their minds with the fables, even more than they shape their bodies with the hand."

Upon the broad principles here formulated the value of the children's rooms depends. For it will be conceded that the two requisites of a library are to place good books upon the shelves and to see that they are read.

In the first section of this chapter, the individual promptings of a conscientious person were suggested; but a more systematic method of book-selection should be adopted, whereby a book is chosen because it has passed scrutiny of a committee elected for the special purpose. In order to protect the average demand, such a board should, of necessity, be a body catholic in taste, and not wholly academic in tone. It should bear in mind that a consulting library is different in function and in appeal from the general circulating branches; that the specialised critic must pass, not always upon whether there is sufficient fact in the book, but upon whether what fact there is has been dealt with truly, rather than fully

As early as 1893, Paul Ziegler established a German monthly, the *Jugendschriftenwarte*, in which he purposed to teach the German people how to examine children's books, classical and modern. He believed firmly that he would be able to reach some scientific basis, some consistent standard, which would be founded upon psychological, pedagogical, and æsthetic experience. This ambitious beginning by Ziegler led to the organisation of committees for the same purpose. In 1900, there were twenty-six centres throughout the Empire engaged in the study, and they were soon gathered together by Heinrich Wolgast,[55] a specialist on the subject of children's reading, into a "union" called "Die vereinigten deutschen Prüfungsausschüsse für Jugendschriften."

By 1906, the movement had so grown that seventy-eight local committees, with a common interest and a strong organisation, were working in twenty-six German States, their energy being felt and their example being followed in Austria, Switzerland, and France.

These committees have been weeding out, according to their æsthetic, educational, and national ideals, all undesirable literature for children, leaving nothing but the best. It would appear that in the course of their examination they called into account the opinions of parent, teacher, librarian, author, illustrator, and publisher. The local committees, working in hearty sympathy with the local libraries, had but one watchword, *excellent*; the book was read three times by a number of committees—sometimes as many as six, when the book would pass through eighteen hands. If a committee's decision was unanimous, the result was sent to the central office of the confederation; if there was a difference of opinion, an arbitrator was called in.

Miss Isabel Chadburn, in a suggestive article,[56] quotes fully some of the final reports which are always sent to the *Jugendschriftenwarte* for publication. Here is one dealing summarily with a book:

"'The Lifeboat,' Ballantyne (From the English of). Four pictures in colour, black-and-white illustrations in the text; second edition; 8vo, 122 pages. Leipzig: Otto Spamer, 1892. Price 1 m.

"Tested by: Berlin (no); Breslau (no); Halle (no); Königsberg (yes); Posen (no); Stettin (yes).

"A story of adventure in which the interest of the reader is directly excited through the keeping up of a succession of extraordinary events. The characterisation is utterly superficial and contradictory. The style, hard to understand on account of the numerous technical nautical terms, is full of indistinct and distorted metaphors and expressions. The pictures are crude and badly drawn. Upon these grounds the book is rejected."

By the German method, a poor book would find small chances of surviving. Already this test has met with opposition from the German "Union of Booksellers, Selling on a Commission." But the crusade is steadily gaining ground and the influence having effect.

The academic tone detected in this plan is its one objection. Were the same policy adopted in America, it would only add to an already over-conscious education-getting process. As we seem to be obsessed by the idea, far better it would be simply to trust to a general impression of a book, than to have it squeezed and analysed out of existence. A teacher who served on such a board would be obliged to cut herself completely adrift from the school-room atmosphere, and to criticise from a cultural standpoint, tempered by her educational experience.

We have our own children to consider; European States are sending us theirs. It is no small matter to decide what they should read. In the library, the juvenile member is to find a full and free development. Russian and Polish, French, German and Italian, Yiddish and English—all these must be satisfied. But there is one thing positive; however conglomerate the membership, a library for children must assume as a fundamental maxim that the best books alone will create the best taste.

We shall be obliged to come to it sooner or later,—a guillotine method—the wholesale eviction of all literature which is an outgrowth of this attempt to drag our classics down, in order to appeal condescendingly to youthful intellects, and to foreshorten our fiction so as to satisfy a trivial mood. Wisely, the librarian is moving by degrees; a sudden adoption of a rigorous standard would find an army of readers wholly unprepared; the ideal must be made to suit the needs of different environments. Whatever rules are formulated to hasten the improvement, they must be pliable and not fixed; for, though all localities may be improving, this betterment will be found to vary in degree with each section.

Having stacked the shelves, the next step is to appeal to the child through suggestion; to find out, as well as opportunity will permit, wherein his tastes lie, and what class of book dominates his card, as seen by the catalogue notation stamped upon it. The librarian must seek to divert any miscarriage of energy; to lead away from undesirable tendencies by gradual substitution of something a little higher in motive and much stronger in style. She must resort to exciting subterfuges: the bulletin accessory, the book-lists, the story hour—in fact, whatever her inventive mind can shape to awaken interest, to foster a desire for something above the average taste.

There are some who approve of closing the shelves to children, and in this way of directing the distribution of books to the individual. Not only is this impracticable, but it deprives a child of that personal contact with all kinds of books by means of which he is to learn his own inclination. We must infer that all books upon the juvenile shelves are placed there because they are thought suitable for children. The librarian may reserve that prerogative of concealing a book and regarding it out, should a demand for it come from one who should not, for any apparent reason, have it. But the jurisdiction of the librarian over the child-taste, just as the jurisdiction of the teacher over the child-mind, ends where the home is expected to proclaim its effectiveness and its right.

IV. THE EXPERIMENTAL TEMPTATION.

Many attempts have been made to treat statistically the reading tastes of children, but the results are significant only in a few details, and even these vary from locality to locality, as they differ from child to child. The psychology of sex becomes apparent by the manner in which boys and girls respond to the same stimulus. But we ought not to place much value upon a canvass of this kind, for the answers that are sent to any class of questions are more or less artificial, in many cases reflecting some grown person's estimate of a book. It is important for the librarian to know the proportions in which fiction and non-fiction are circulated, and what books are in greatest demand. The temperature changes of taste need thus to be followed. But history deals with crucial moments.

Every one interested in the subject of juvenile reading has tried to experiment and has received quaint answers to stereotyped questions—answers filled with humour, now and then with a spontaneous exclamation of appreciation. In my own case, some four hundred letters were sent to me from children, North and South. They showed me local variations in reading tastes; they showed me educational weaknesses, such as a general mechanical study of a few hackneyed poems; they showed me an indiscriminate reading, by the fourteen- or fifteen-year-old girl, of fiction such as Besant's "Children of Gideon" and Mrs. Humphry Ward's "Fenwick's Career." Furthermore, they pointed in some instances to individual tastes; and most of them indicated a dire confusion as to the meaning of the terms *fiction* and *non-fiction*.

By such an experiment, however, one begins to realise how rich the field of juvenile energy is—a stream of voluntary desire seeking some course to the sea. From a multitude of such letters one may comprehend why the librarian insists on proceeding slowly in order to counteract deficiencies. The newsboy, without his five-cent weekly, still must have his penny-dreadful classic; the girl, too old for the juvenile book, must be furnished with a transitional book on the way to the grown-up shelves; our foreign children must be encouraged to read, according to the librarian's idea, something different from themselves, something not of their own environment.[57]

We were warned by the writer in the *Quarterly Review* not to regard the extremes of genius or of dulness, in estimating children. And yet, biography is filled with that appealing detail of juvenile taste, which the grown person delights in recording. Lamb's remembrance of the Stackhouse Bible, Coleridge's dreamy dread of the Arabian Nights, Scott's lusty shouting of the ballad of Hardy Knute, Tennyson's spreading his arms to the sky and chanting, "I hear a voice that's speaking in the wind," Stevenson's crooning to himself in the dark his "songstries"[58]—these touches do not betoken the genius of men, but the genius of childhood. Whenever we find such young people brought in contact with children's literature, they do not relish the experience; they recognise as of value only that which they can but partially comprehend, yet which is told out of the depths of a writer's heart and understanding. They respond to the spirit of great literature from their earliest moments; for its sake, they overcome the sensitiveness of temperament which nowadays must be in so far reckoned with that all causes for fear are rejected from a story. To them, there is a certain educative value in fear. Coleridge, timourous as he was when not more than six, devoured the gilt-covered books of Jack-the-Giant-Killer and of Tom Hickathrift, whom Thackeray delighted in, not because he was so tall, but because he was so *thick*; and though it is said that his father burnt many of these nerve-exacting tales, we hear Coleridge exclaiming during the course of a lecture delivered in 1811:

"Give me the works which delighted my youth! Give me the History of St. George and the Seven Champions of Christendom, which at every leisure moment I used to hide myself in a corner to read! Give me the Arabian Nights' Entertainments, which I used to watch, till the sun shining on the book-case approached, and, glowing full upon it, gave me the courage to take it from the shelf."[59]

We interpret these remarks in terms of genius, without giving the average mind credit for such opinions, just because they are left unrecorded. Every child has his night fears and his day dreams, however regulated they may be by his social environment. These vary in degree according to the intellectual energy and spiritual refinement fostered in each one of us. The librarian's problem is based upon an acknowledgment of this potential energy and refinement; she reckons with the child's voluntary interest. For all childhood is seeking to find expression in numberless ways; its eye for the first time sees the outline of life, its voice expresses for the first time the rhythm of its nature in song. Its compass in all things is small, but its timbre is pure.

FOOTNOTES

[47] The general complaint among librarians is that these picture-books of the best type are too rare and too expensive to purchase in large quantities for general circulation.

[48] Read Stevenson's "A Penny Plain" in Memories and Portraits; also "The Dime Novel in American Life," by Charles M. Harvey, *Atlantic*, 100:37 (July, 1907).

[49] By Archdeacon Wilberforce, Hannah More's friend.

[50] *Vide* "Reading for Boys and Girls," by Everett T. Tomlinson. *Atlantic*, 86:693 (Nov., 1900).

[51] Article on Children's Books. Reprinted in *Living Age*, Aug. 10, 1844, 2:1.

[52] There was the Elliptical Questioning—a form of "drawing out" and "injecting" knowledge and information.

[53] In a letter to the author, Mr. C. G. Leland, Superintendent of the Bureau of Libraries, New York Board of Education, plainly states the province and the mission of the school library. He writes: "Nearly all of our educational institutions nowadays are very busily engaged in supplying *useful information*. The practical is crowding everything else out of their courses of study. The kind of knowledge that will help in the future struggle for existence and material betterment is being demanded more and more and is being taught to the exclusion of much that is only ethical or cultural.

"As a continual protest against this materialistic tendency the school library takes its position and marshals its books. Its first purpose is to create a love for good literature and beautiful pictures as soon as the child has mastered the mechanics of reading; its ultimate aim is culture.

"In the elementary school the library should reach to every class-room and offer there a few very attractive and very carefully selected books, so attractive and so well graded that the most indifferent boy or girl will be led by easy stages into the green fields of literature.

"The class-room is still the strategic point, for even homes of refinement are wont to delegate the work of directing the children's reading to the school, and the teacher with her case of well-known books has every day opportunities denied to public librarian and to the majority of parents.

"The school library naturally points the way to the public library; its relation to that institution is that of the preparatory school to the university.

"In supplying reference-books, and in correlating a certain amount of recreative reading with the school course, the library has another important field, but one which should be subordinated to the larger and broader function."

[54] This involves a careful consideration of a juvenile reference library.

[55] Heinrich Wolgast, the German authority, has written: "Vom Kinderbuch," Leipzig, Teubner, 1906.

[56] *Vide* London *Library Association Record*, Feb. 15, 1907.

[57] This last statement, however, may be refuted by the répertoire of a Yiddish theatre. I have witnessed the theme of "King Lear" applied to Jewish life, and followed with bated breath by the boy in the gallery.

[58] Stevenson's father once stood outside the door and recorded one of these impromptu poems. The Rev. Charles Kingsley, when a boy, is said to have done the same thing.

[59] *Vide* W. M. Rossetti's Memoirs of Dante Gabriel Rossetti. Chap. VI, Childish Book Reading and Scribbling.

VI.
APPENDIX

I. Book-lists Published by Libraries.

What principle of selection shall one adopt in making a book-list? No hard and fast rules can be framed, for what I may consider best may be rejected as second best by you. There is not a book-list issued that does not differ from the others in many essentials; in classification, in titles, and in purpose. Most of these lists are marked by a sincere effort on the part of librarians to direct a child's reading along the best lines. But even though they may be suggestive and helpful, at the most they are passive and need to be supplemented by a personal knowledge of the books recommended. For, in the lists of history and biography, a compiler finds it necessary to adopt many volumes that are far from literary in the style of writing or in the manner of treatment. To-morrow these books may give place to others far superior and far more permanent in value.

The agreement between the lists, however, does show that there are numberless stories, legends, and the like, which are generally acceded to be desirable, as much because of their inherent freshness as because of the fact that they have stood the test of time. Rarely do the lists fail to mention them.

Notwithstanding, the recommendations issued by the libraries usually are sent forth, hedged around by exceptions and by indirect warnings. This is a healthful sign; it indicates that, however intent the maker of book-lists may be to offer the best, human nature is not all of the same calibre, and excellence is of an illusive character.

It is with some peculiar pleasure that I offer the list of books in this Appendix, protecting myself, and the committee that aided me, with excuses, and forestalling criticism by claiming that while the recommendations have been made to the best of several abilities, and in accord with no mean standards of selection—at the same time much has been included of necessity which will pass away in the years to come. This is not an exclusive list; the attempt has been made to have it a practical, workable list, for parents and teachers and librarians to consult, bringing to it their own personal judgment as to individual taste and development of the child under consideration. Such a term as "the child" has been used reluctantly, since there is no other term, more human, less mechanical, to take its place. Because of this dislike for a stereotyped grading of childhood, the reader will here find no indication as to age demands. The books have been mentioned with a generous range of from six to fifteen years.

Other lists will be found to include a fuller division of subjects. Notably in the historical sections, they will contain many more references than are here given. Our histories smack largely of the school-room; they do not differ so very much from each other as to excellence; they are very apt to agree in the zealousness with which they follow fact. If we decide to seek for general literary merit, we should avoid, as far as possible, the inclusion of what we know is not the case; of what we know is intended for the class-room.

And so, in order to supplement our method, which may be considered too narrow or too broad, the following table of available lists, which have been brought to my notice, is included:

BOOK-LISTS

A. L. A. ANNOTATED LISTS—Books for Boys and Girls. A Selected List Compiled by Caroline M. Hewins, Librarian of the Hartford Public Library. 1904. $0.15. A most judicious and literary standard.

A LIST OF BOOKS RECOMMENDED FOR A CHILDREN'S LIBRARY—Compiled for the Iowa Library Commission by Annie Carroll Moore, Supervisor of Children's Rooms in the New York City Public Library. Another excellent and practical guide.

BOOKS FOR BOYS—Special Bulletin No. 6. January, 1906. The Chicago Public Library. A generous selection for boys from twelve to eighteen; an inclusive list, marked more by vigour than by refinement of a fastidious nature.

FINGERPOSTS TO CHILDREN'S READING—Walter Taylor Field. McClurg, $1.00. The book contains some practical suggestions about children and their reading. The lists in the Appendix are open to criticism.

THE RIGHT READING FOR CHILDREN—Compiled by Charles Welsh. Heath. Referring chiefly to Heath's Home and School Classics.

STORY TELLING TO CHILDREN FROM NORSE MYTHOLOGY AND THE NIBELUNGENLIED—References to Material on Selected Stories, Together with an Annotated Reading List. Carnegie Library, Pittsburgh. $0.20. Excellent.

STORY HOUR COURSES FOR CHILDREN FROM GREEK MYTHS, THE ILIAD, AND THE ODYSSEY, as Conducted by the Children's Department of the Carnegie Library of Pittsburgh. $0.05. An excellent guide.

A LIST OF GOOD STORIES TO TELL TO CHILDREN UNDER TWELVE YEARS OF AGE, with a Brief Account of the Story Hour Conducted by the

Children's Department, Carnegie Library, Pittsburgh. $0.05. The same Library has issued:

ANNOTATED CATALOGUE OF BOOKS USED IN THE HOME LIBRARIES AND READING CLUBS, conducted by the Children's Department. $0.25.

BOOKS FOR CHILDREN—A List Compiled by Gertrude Wild Arnold. The Marion Press, New York. 1905.

READING FOR THE YOUNG—Sargent. Houghton.

A CHILDREN'S LIBRARY—Selected by May H. Prentice and Effie L. Power, in behalf of the Cleveland Normal School.

CATALOGUE OF BOOKS FOR PUBLIC SCHOOL LIBRARIES IN NEW YORK—Compiled by Claude G. Leland. Marked by educational requirements, and graded.

A LIST OF BOOKS ON BIRDS for the General Reader and Students. Audubon Society of the State of New York. Recommended by Mr. Frank M. Chapman, of the New York Museum of Natural History. *Vide* "Bird-Lore," a magazine which Mr. Chapman edits.

CHILDREN'S REFERENCE LISTS—Cleveland Public Library. English History for the Sixth Grade. The system here adopted is excellent, and might be followed with advantage in other lines.

CHILDREN, SCHOOLS, AND LIBRARIES—A list, with abstracts, of some of the more important contributions to the subject. Compiled by Marion Dickinson in 1897; revised by Mary Medlicott in 1899. Springfield Public Library. Springfield, Massachusetts. A very serviceable pamphlet.

FIVE HUNDRED BOOKS FOR THE YOUNG—George E. Hardy. Scribner.

SOME ENGLISH CATALOGUES recommended by Miss Isabel Chadburn:

a. Catalogue of Books for Secondary Schools.

b. Prize List, Education Committee, London County Council. Graded.

c. Buckingham Palace Road Library. Mr. Pacy.

d. Cable Street, Stepney, E., Library. Mr. Roebuck.

e. Descriptive Handbook to Juvenile Literature. Finsbury Public Libraries, Mr. Cannons.

f. Group of Books for Schools. Librarian of the Cardiff Library. Mr. Ballinger.

As far as nature books are concerned, it will be found that local differences have to be observed; yet, though the British and American writers are bound to these limitations, they are none the less alike in their scope—to furnish the juvenile readers with a ready reference guide to objects around them. In the present instance, the list which has been compiled, voted upon, and arranged, may suit the English child as well as the American child, although certain local inclusions need to be balanced by the substitution of English counterparts. The American school story, *per se*, will never supplant its English predecessor in "Tom Brown at Rugby," or even "The Crofton Boys." The American library shelves are stacked with the English make of book. And it must be acknowledged that, in point of scholarship, the English classics, given a library and literary *format*, surpass the school-book shape in every way. In this connection, it is well to heed the warning of Miss Moore:

"The choice of editions is not based upon extended comparative work. [What is said of her list applies as well to the present one.] It represents merely the editions which have come to my notice, some of them being quite unsatisfactory. This is an era of educational publications and, while many of these are admirably adapted to their purpose, we have need to be constantly on our guard not to overstock children's libraries with books which have no artistic merit as to cover or general make-up, and which therefore fail to make a definite individual impression on the mind of the child and give to a children's library the general appearance of book-shelves devoted to supplementary reading."

Were this intended to be an exclusive list, many very rigourous omissions would have been the result; but it is better to err upon the generous side than to appeal to an exceptional taste. "A man's reach should exceed his grasp" is the Browning philosophy, but in the climb upward the intermediate tendrils are necessary for holding on; nor must they be removed until something is assured to take their place. The removal of inferior books from the shelves will not remedy the matter, unless existing circumstances are such as to meet the case.

Where it is possible, the least expensive edition has been adopted; although it is often a fact that no choice has been given. A good edition for a library is the most desirable, and those committees are unwise which sacrifice quality for quantity. On the other hand, it is unfortunate that a more suitable arrangement cannot exist, whereby the artistic books, which, by reason of their decorative character, are perforce expensive, could be offered at less exorbitant rates to an institution of such social importance as a library.

II. A LIST OF SELECTED BOOKS FOR CHILDREN.
PICTURE-BOOKS AND PICTURES

(The NISTER PICTURE-BOOKS are sold in this country by DUTTON.)

BEDFORD, FRANCES D.—Book of Shops. (Verses by E. V. Lucas.) Dutton, $2.50.

BRADLEY, WILL—Peter Poodle, Toy Maker to the King. Dodd, $1.50 net.

CALDECOTT, RANDOLPH—Toy Books. Warne, (4 vols.) $1.25 each. The separate stories are sold at $0.25 each, and comprise, among a large number, the following: The Farmer's Boy; A Frog He Would A-Wooing Go; Hey Diddle Diddle and Baby Bunting; The House That Jack Built; The Milk Maid; The Queen of Hearts; Ride a Cock Horse; Sing a Song of Sixpence; John Gilpin.

COX, PALMER—The Brownie Books. Century, $1.50 each.

CRANE, WALTER—Mother Hubbard's Picture Book. Lane, $1.25.

This Little Pig's Picture Book. Lane, $1.25. [There are other volumes. Crane also ill. Lamb's fanciful essay, "The Masque of Days." Cassell, $2.50.]

Mother Hubbard; This Little Pig; Aladdin; Beauty and the Beast; Bluebeard; The Forty Thieves; The Frog Prince; Goody Two Shoes; Sleeping Beauty; The Fairy Ship; Baby's A B C. Lane, $0.25 each.

DE MONVEL, BOUTET—Filles et Garçons. (Stories by Anatole France.) Hachette; Brentano, $2.35.

Chansons de France pour les petits Français. Hachette; Plon, $2.50.

La Civilité puérile et honnête. Plon; Brentano, $2.35.

Nos Enfants. (Text by Anatole France.) Hachette; Brentano, $1.25.

Fables de La Fontaine, choisies pour les enfants. S. P. C. K.; Brentano, $2.35.

GERSON, VIRGINIA—Happy Heart Family. Duffield, $1.00. (There is a second volume.)

GREENAWAY, KATE—A Day in a Child's Life. (Music, verse, pictures.) Warne, $1.50.

Marigold Garden. Routledge (Warne, $1.50), $2.00.

Under the Window. (Pictures and Rhymes.) Warne, $1.50.

A Apple Pie, etc. Warne, $0.75.

Mother Goose. Warne, $0.75.

Mavor's Spelling Book. Warne, $0.40.

GUIGOU, P. ET VIMAR, A.—L'illustre Dompteur. (The French Circus Book.) Plon; Brentano, $2.35.

HOFFMANN, HEINRICH—Slovenly Peter. Coates, $1.50. [German editions are preferable.]

PERKINS, LUCY FITCH—Adventures of Robin Hood. Stokes, $1.50.

WHITCOMB, IDA P.—Young People's Story of Art. Dodd, $2.00. [Sarah Tytler is the author of "The Old Masters and their Pictures"; "Modern Painters and Their Paintings." Little, Brown, $1.50 each. *Vide* Poetry; also German section, Richter, etc. The French are here included since they are so familiar to English readers.]

MYTHS, FOLK-LORE, LEGENDS, FAIRY TALES, AND HERO TALES

ÆSOP—Fables. (Tr., Joseph Jacobs.) Macmillan, $1.50.

A Hundred Fables of Æsop. (Tr., Sir Roger L'Estrange; intro., Kenneth Grahame.) Lane, $1.50 net.

The Babies' Own. (Ill., Walter Crane.) Warne, $1.50.

ANDERSEN, H. C.—Fairy Tales. (Tr., H. L. Braekstad; ill., Tegner; 2 vols.) Century, $5.00. Fairy Tales. (Tr., Mrs. Edgar Lucas.) Macmillan, $0.50; Dent, $2.50. [Ill., the Robinsons. *Vide* also Contes Choisis, Bibliothèque Rose.]

ARABIAN NIGHTS' ENTERTAINMENTS—(Ed., Andrew Lang.) Longmans, $2.00.

Fairy Tales From. (Ed., E. Dixon.) Dent, 2 vols., 7s. 6d. net each.

ASBJÖRNSEN, P. C.—Fairy Tales From the Far North. Armstrong, $2.00; Burt, $1.00. [Folk and Fairy Tales. Tr., H. L. Braekstad; intro., E. W. Gosse.]

BALDWIN, JAMES—The Story of Siegfried. (Ill., Pyle.) Scribner, $1.50.

The Story of Roland. (Ill., Birch.) Scribner, $1.50.

BROWN, ABBIE FARWELL—The Book of Saints and Friendly Beasts. Houghton, $1.25.

In the Days of Giants. Houghton, $1.10 net.

BULFINCH, THOMAS—The Age of Fable. Lothrop, Lee, $1.50. [Cheaper editions, Altemus, Crowell, etc.]

CANTOR, WILLIAM—True Annals of Fairyland. Reign of King Herla. (Ill., Charles Robinson.) Dent, 4s. 6d. net.

CARROLL, LEWIS—Alice's Adventures in Wonderland. (Ill., Sir John Tenniel.) Macmillan, $1.00. [There is also an edition, Harper, ill., by Peter Newell, $3.00 net. The reader is advised to consult Mr. Dodgson's Life and Letters.]

Through the Looking-Glass and What Alice Found There. (Ill., Sir John Tenniel. Sequel to the above.) Macmillan, $1.00.

CHAPIN, A. A.—Story of the Rhinegold. Harper, $1.25. [*Vide* also "Wonder Tales from Wagner." She is the author of "Masters of Music." Dodd, $1.50.]

CHURCH, A. J.—Charlemagne and the Twelve Peers of France. Macmillan, $1.75.

CRUIKSHANK, GEORGE—The Cruikshank Fairy Book. Putnam, $1.25; $2.00.

FRANCILLON, R. E.—Gods and Heroes. Ginn, $0.40.

GIBBON, J. M. (ED.)—True Annals of Fairyland. Reign of King Cole. (Ill., Charles Robinson.) Macmillan, $2.00.

GRIMM, J. L. AND W. K.—Fairy Tales of the Brothers. (Tr., Mrs. Edgar Lucas; ill., Arthur Rackham.) Lippincott, $2.50; $1.50. [Editions also ill., Cruikshank; intro., Ruskin,—Chatto and Windus, 6s.; Macmillan, ill., Walter Crane, $1.50; Contes Choisis; Bibliothèque Rose; *vide* German section.]

HARRIS, JOEL CHANDLER—Uncle Remus and His Friends. (Ill., Frost.) Houghton, $1.50.

Nights with Uncle Remus. (Ill., Church.) Houghton, $1.50.

Uncle Remus: His Songs and His Sayings. (Ill., Frost.) Appleton, $2.00

HAWTHORNE, NATHANIEL—A Wonderbook for Girls and Boys. (Ill., Walter Crane.) Houghton, $3.00.

Tanglewood Tales. (Ill., G. W. Edwards.) Houghton, $1.00; $2.50.

HORNE, RICHARD HENGIST—The Good-Natured Bear. [Out of print, but re-publication is strongly recommended by librarians.]

INGELOW, JEAN—Mopsa, the Fairy. Little, Brown, $1.25.

IRVING, WASHINGTON—Rip Van Winkle and The Legend of Sleepy Hollow. Macmillan, $1.50. [Expensive illustrated editions issued by Putnam and Doubleday.]

JACOBS, JOSEPH—English Fairy Tales. Putnam, $1.25.

The Most Delectable History of Reynard the Fox. Macmillan, $1.50.

Book of Wonder Voyages. Macmillan, $1.50.

Celtic Fairy Tales. Putnam, $1.25.

KINGSLEY, CHARLES—The Heroes; or, Greek Fairy Tales for My Children. (Ill., T. H. Robinson.) Dutton, $2.50. [*Vide* also editions Crowell; Harper, $2.50.]

The Water Babies. Macmillan, $1.25. [Cheaper Editions.]

KIPLING, RUDYARD—Just-So Stories. Doubleday, $1.20 net. [There is also a "Just-So Song Book," $1.20 net.]

Jungle Book. (First and second series.) Century, $1.50 each.

Puck of Pook's Hill. (Ill., Arthur Rackham.) Doubleday, $1.50.

LABOULAYE, E. R. L. DE—Fairy Tales. Routledge, $1.25; Harper, $2.00.

The Last Fairy Tales. Harper, $2.00.

LA FONTAINE—Selected Fables. (Ill., Boutet de Monvel.) Young, $2.50.

LANG, ANDREW (ED.)—The Red Fairy Book. Longmans, $2.00.

The Blue Fairy Book. Longmans, $2.00.

The Book of Romance. Longmans, $1.60 net.

LANIER, SIDNEY—The Boy's King Arthur. Scribner, $2.00. [Lanier bases his narrative on Mallory. *Vide* Howard Pyle's "Story of King Arthur and His Knights." Scribner, $2.50.]

The Boy's Froissart. Scribner, $2.00.

Knightly Tales of Wales; or, The Boy's Mabinogion. Scribner, $2.00.

The Boy's Percy. [Full introduction and the ballads based on original.] Scribner, $2.00.

MABIE, H. W.—Norse Stories. Dodd, $1.80 net.

MACDONALD, GEORGE—At the Back of the North Wind. Routledge, $1.25; Burt, $1.00.

MULOCK-CRAIK, DINAH M.—The Fairy Book. Macmillan, $1.00.

The Adventures of a Brownie. Harper, $0.60; Page, $0.50.

The Little Lame Prince. Harper, $0.60.

MUSSET, PAUL DE—Mr. Wind and Madam Rain. Putnam, $2.00. [*Vide* Petite Bibliothèque Blanche.]

PERRAULT, CHARLES—Fairy Tales. Macmillan, $0.40 net. [*Vide* p. 36.]

PYLE, HOWARD—Merry Adventures of Robin Hood. Scribner, $3.00. [An excellent version of the ballad has been issued by Stokes, ill., Lucy Fitch Perkins.]

RUSKIN, JOHN—King of the Golden River. Ginn, $0.25; Page, $0.50.

SCUDDER, HORACE E. (COMPILER.)—Book of Legends. Houghton, $0.50.

STOCKTON, FRANK R.—The Queen's Museum and Other Fanciful Tales. Scribner, $2.50. [*Vide* former edition, "Clocks of Rondaine and other stories." Scribner, $1.50.]

THACKERAY, W. M.—The Rose and the Ring. Putnam, $0.50, $1.00. [*Vide* other editions.]

POETRY AND VERSE

ALLINGHAM, WILLIAM—The Ballad Book. Macmillan, $1.00.

BLAKE, WILLIAM—Songs of Innocence. (Ill., Geraldine Morris.) Lane, $0.50 net.

BROWNING, ROBERT—The Pied Piper of Hamelin. (Ill., Kate Greenaway.) Warne, $1.50.

BURGESS, GELETT—Goops and How to be Them. (Several volumes.) Stokes, $1.50.

CARY, ALICE AND PHŒBE—Ballads for Little Folks. Houghton, $1.50.

CHILD, LYDIA MARIA—Flowers for Children; New Flowers for Children. [Out of print, but re-publication is strongly recommended by librarians.]

DODGE, MARY MAPES (ED.)—Baby Days. Century, $1.50.

ENGLISH AND SCOTTISH POPULAR BALLADS. (Ed., Sargent-Kittredge, from Francis James Child's collection, Cambridge edition.) Houghton, $3.00.

FIELD, EUGENE—Poems of Childhood. (Ill., Maxfield Parrish.) Scribner, $2.50.

GOLDSMITH, OLIVER—The Deserted Village. (Ill., E. A. Abbey.) Harper, $3.00. [Abbey also illustrated "She Stoops to Conquer," $5.00.]

HENLEY, W. E. (COMPILER)—Lyra Heroica: A Book of Verses for Boys. Scribner, $1.25.

HOLMES, OLIVER W.—Poems. (Complete ed., Cambridge.) Houghton, $2.00, $1.50. [*Vide* "The One Hoss Shay," ill., Howard Pyle, $1.50.]

JERROLD, WALTER (ED.)—The Big Book of Nursery Rhymes. Dutton, $3.00.

LAMB, CHARLES AND MARY—Poetry for Children. (Ill., Winifred Green; pref., I. Gollancz.) Dent, 2s. 6d. net. [*Vide* in same edition "Mrs. Leicester's School," 5s. net.]

LANG, ANDREW (ED.)—The Blue Poetry Book. Longmans, $2.00.

LEAR, EDWARD—Nonsense Books. Little, Brown, $2.00. [*Vide* also Warne edition.]

LONGFELLOW, HENRY W.—Poems. (Complete ed., Cambridge.) Houghton, $2.00. [*Vide* also "Hiawatha," ill., Remington, $4.00.]

LOWELL, JAMES R.—The Vision of Sir Launfal. Houghton, $1.50.

LUCAS, E. V. (ED.)—A Book of Verses for Children. Holt, $2.00. [There is a school edition.]

MACAULAY, T. B.—Lays of Ancient Rome. Longmans, $1.25. [*Vide* editions Houghton, Putnam.]

MATTHEWS, BRANDER—Poems of American Patriotism. Scribner, $1.50. [*Vide* "English History Told by English Poets." Ed., Bates and Coman. Macmillan, $0.60 net.]

MOTHER GOOSE NURSERY RHYMES (Ill., Tenniel, Crane, etc.)—Dutton, $1.50. [*Vide* Nister ed., Routledge, etc.]

MOTHER GOOSE'S MELODIES—Houghton, $1.50.

NORTON, C. E. (ED.)—Heart of Oak Books. Heath, 7 vols., from $0.25 to $0.60. [Collection of Rhymes, Poems, Stories, etc.]

PALGRAVE, F. T.—The Children's Treasury of English Song. Macmillan, $1.00.

PATMORE, COVENTRY (ED.)—Children's Garland from the Best Poets. Macmillan, $1.00.

REPPLIER, AGNES (ED.)—Book of Famous Verse. Houghton, $0.75 and $1.25.

RILEY, JAMES WHITCOMB—Rhymes of Childhood. Bobbs-Merrill, $1.25.

ROSSETTI, CHRISTINA G.—Sing-Song. Macmillan, $1.50.

SCOTT, SIR WALTER—Marmion; The Lay of the Last Minstrel. (Ed., W. J. Rolfe.) Houghton, $0.75 each.

SHUTE, KATHARINE H. AND DUNTON, LARKIN (COMPILERS)—The Land of Song. Silver, 3 vols., $0.36 to $0.54.

STEVENSON, ROBERT L.—A Child's Garden of Verses. Scribner. (Ill., Robinson, $1.50; ill., Jessie W. Smith, $2.50.) [An excellent, inexpensive edition, Rand, McNally, $0.75.]

TAYLOR, JANE AND ANN—Little Ann and Other Poems. (Ill., Kate Greenaway). Warne, $1.00. [*Vide* also edition, ed., E. V. Lucas. Stokes, $1.50. Including verses of Adelaide O'Keeffe; ill., F. D. Bedford. *Vide* "Greedy Dick and Other Stories in Verse," by the Taylors, $0.50.]

TENNYSON, ALFRED, LORD—Selected Poems for Young People. (Ed., W. J. Rolfe.) Houghton, $0.75. [Children should be made acquainted with parts of the "Idylls of the King."]

WATTS, ISAAC—Childhood Songs of Long Ago. Wessels, $0.75. [*Vide* English editions.]

WELSH, CHARLES—Book of Nursery Rhymes. (Edited and graded.) Heath, $0.30. [In Home and School Classics.]

WIGGIN, K. D., AND SMITH, N. A. (EDS.)—Golden Numbers: A Book of Verse for Youth. McClure, $2.00 net.

Posy Ring: A Book of Verse for Children. McClure, $1.25 net. [The same editors have gathered together a book of nursery rhymes.]

CLASSICS

CERVANTES, MIGUEL DE—Don Quixote of the Mancha. (Retold by Judge E. A. Parry; ill., Walter Crane.) Lane, $1.50.

CHAUCER, GEOFFREY—Canterbury Tales. (Retold by Percy MacKaye; ill., W. Appleton Clark.) Duffield, $2.50.

Canterbury Chimes; or, Chaucer Tales Retold to Children. Storr, Frances and Turner, Hawes. Kegan, Paul, 3s. 6d.

Chaucer for Children. Mrs. H. R. Haweis. Scribner, $1.25.

CHURCH, A. H.—Lords of the World. (Pictures from Roman Life and Story). Appleton, $1.50.

HERODOTUS—Wonder Stories from. Told by Boden, G. H., and D'Almeida, W. B. Harper, $2.50.

HOMER—Iliad. (Tr., W. C. Bryant.) Houghton, $1.00 to $9.00. [*Vide* also tr., Lang, Leaf, Myers.]

LAMB, CHARLES—The Adventures of Ulysses. Harper, $2.50. [*Vide* also ed., E. V. Lucas, Putnam.]

ODYSSEUS, ADVENTURES OF—(Retold by Marvin, F. S., and others; ill., Charles Robinson.) Dutton, $1.50. [*Vide* also ed., G. H. Palmer and W. C. Perry.]

PLUTARCH—Lives. [Full ed.; also J. S. White's "Boys' and Girls' Plutarch." Putnam, $1.75.]

SHAKESPEARE—Girlhood of Shakespeare's Heroines. Mary Cowden Clarke. (Ill., Sir John Gilbert.) Scribner, $3.00.

Tales from. Charles and Mary Lamb. Macmillan, $1.00. (Ed., Ainger.) [*Vide* also ed., E. V. Lucas, Putnam; ed. ill., Norman M. Price, Scribner; ed. Nister. Quiller Couch has treated the historical tales in the same manner. Scribner.]

SWIFT, JONATHAN—Gulliver's Travels. Macmillan, $1.25 net.

TOWRY, M. H.—Spenser for Children. Scribner, $1.25.

"HOW TO DO THINGS"—AMUSEMENTS

ALCOTT, L. M.—Little Women Play. (Adapted from the story by E. L. Gould.) Little, Brown, $0.50.

BEARD, DAN—The Field and Forest Handy Book. Scribner, $2.00.

The Jack of All Trades. Scribner, $2.00.

The American Boy's Handy Book. Scribner, $2.00.

BEARD, L. AND A.—Things Worth Doing and How to Do Them. Scribner, $2.00.

Handicraft and Recreation for Girls. Scribner. $2.00.

BLACK, ALEXANDER—Photography Indoors and Out. Houghton, $1.25.

Boys, C. V.—Soap Bubbles and the Forces Which Made Them. Gorham, $0.75.

Cutter, Mrs. S. J. (Compiler.)—Conundrums, Riddles, Puzzles, and Games. Hansauer.

Games Book for Boys and Girls. Dutton, $2.50. (*Vide* Nister.)

Kelley, L. E.—Three Hundred Things a Bright Girl Can Do. Estes, $1.75.

King, G. G.—Comedies and Legends for Marionettes. Macmillan, $1.50.

Lewis, A. J. (Prof. Hoffman.)—Magic at Home. Cassell, $1.25. [*Vide* also "Modern Magic." Routledge, $1.50.]

Lucas, E. V. and Elizabeth—What Shall We Do Now? Stokes, $2.00.

Newell, Peter—Topsys and Turvys. Century, $1.00 net.

Seton, Ernest Thompson—The Wild Animal Play. Doubleday, $0.50.

Syrett, Netta—Six Fairy Plays for Children. Lane, $1.00 net.

White, Mary—How to Make Baskets. Doubleday, $1.00 net. [The same author has written a second volume. Many workers prefer "Cane Basket Work." Annie Firth. London: Gill; New York: Milton Bradley.]

MUSIC

In the preparation of this music bibliography, it is a rare privilege to be able to include a list which was compiled by the late Miss Mary L. Avery, of the music department of the Lenox Library, New York; and which was used in a lecture delivered by her before the Pratt Institute Library School on January 12, 1900. To this, the following supplementary list, based upon recommendation, may be added. Prices vary.

Brainard, H. L. (music), and Sage, Betty (words)—Four Childhood Rhymes. Schirmer; The Boston Music Co.

Coolidge, Elizabeth—Fifteen Mother Goose Melodies. Schirmer. (Music somewhat difficult.)

Fisher, William Armes—Posies from A Child's Garden of Verses. Ditson.

Gaynor, Jessie L. (music), and Riley, C. (words)—Songs of the Child World. Nos. 1, 2. The John Church Co.

Jenks, Harriet S., and Rust, Mabel.—Song Echoes from Child Land. Ditson.

Jordan, Jules—A Life Lesson. (Words by Riley.) Schmidt.

McLaughlin, James M., and Gilchrist, W. W.—Educational Music Course. Teachers' Edition for Elementary Grades. Ginn.

Mother Goose Set to Music. (Elliott, J. W.) Novello. [An edition is published by Houghton, $1.50.]

Riley, Gaynor, Beale—Songs for Children. John Church Co.

Taubert, Wilhelm—Klänge aus der Kinderwelt. Schirmer.

In addition, such names as Eleanor Smith and Harvey Worthington Loomis should not be omitted, as composers who recognise successfully the requirements of children's voices. These requirements cannot be too often reiterated. In a letter to the author, the following was underscored: "A child's song must be written almost entirely in the middle register of the voice—neither too high nor too low. Then there must be a distinct melody for the child's ear to catch readily. And the words must interest the child's mind." In this last respect music-teachers are most emphatic. They appeal for verses that stimulate the imagination, they wish words carefully chosen; in the teaching, they seek for purity of diction, for proper valuation of vowels, consonants, and word-endings.

Miss Avery's Music List. Music in Children's Libraries

Breitkopf Edition Catalogue—Breitkopf and Hartel. New York.

Musical, The, Interests [tastes] of Children—Fanny B. Gates. West Springfield, Mass., 1898. [Reprinted from the *Journal of Pedagogy*, October, 1898.]

Novello's School Music Catalogue (Operettas, etc.)—[Descriptive.] London.

Scribner's Musical Literature List—New York.

Literature of Music

Letters from Great Musicians to Young People—Alathea E. Crawford and Alice Chapin. New York, 1897.

Musicians in Rhyme for Childhood's Time—Crawford and Sill. New York, Schirmer.

STORY OF MAJOR C AND HIS RELATIVES: LESSONS IN HARMONY—Grace S. Duff. New York, 1894.

STORY OF MUSIC AND MUSICIANS—Lucy C. Lillie. New York.

STORY OF THE RHINEGOLD—Chapin.

WAGNER STORY-BOOK—William Henry Frost. New York.

Vocal Music

BABY'S BOUQUET—(Old songs.) Ill., Walter Crane. Routledge.

BABY'S OPERA—(Old songs.) Ill., Walter Crane. Routledge; Warne.

BOOK OF RHYMES AND TUNES—Compiled by Margaret P. Osgood [from German and English]. Boston, 1880.

BOOK OF OLD RHYMES SET TO MUSIC—Walter Crane. Warne, $1.20.

CHILD'S GARDEN OF SONG—Arranged by Wm. L. Tomlins. Chicago, 1895.

CHILD'S GARDEN OF VERSES—12 Songs by Stevenson. Music by Mary Carmichael. London.

CHILD'S GARLAND OF SONGS [From a Child's Garden of Verses.]—R. L. Stevenson. Music by C. Villiers Stanford. London, 1892.

CHILDREN'S SINGING GAMES—Eleanor Withey Willard. Grand Rapids, 1895.

CHILDREN'S SOUVENIR SONG BOOK—Arranged by Wm. L. Tomlins. New York, 1893.

CHRISTMAS (A) DREAM—School Operetta—Moffat. London, Novello.

CHRISTMAS CAROLS ANCIENT AND MODERN—Wm. L. Tomlins. New York, 1897.

CHRISTMAS CAROLS NEW AND OLD—Bramley and Sir John Stainer. Novello; Routledge.

GARLAND OF COUNTRY SONG—(English folk songs.) Arranged by S. Baring Gould and H. F. Sheppard. London, 1895.

KINDERGARTEN CHIMES—Kate Douglas Wiggin. Boston (cop.), 1887.

KINDERLIEDER—Von Carl Reinecke. Leipzig; New York, Schirmer.

KINDER- UND JUGEND-LIEDER (50)—Von Hoffman, V. Stuttgart.

KINDERLIEDER (24)—Gustav Fischer. New York.

KINDERLIEDER-ALBUM—Amalie Felsenthal. Leipzig.

MAY-DAY REVELS (Operetta, Old English style.)—Hawkins and West. London.

MUSIK-BEILAGE ZU KINDERFEST—J. Fischer. Berlin, Bloch.

NATIONAL, PATRIOTIC, AND TYPICAL AIRS OF ALL LANDS, with Copious Notes—John Philip Sousa. Philadelphia, 1890.

OLD MAY DAY (Operetta.)—Shapcott Wensley and F. C. Wood. London.

OLDE ENGLYSHE PASTIMES—F. W. Galpin. (Dances and sports, old music.) London.

SINGING (A) QUADRILLE, SET TO NURSERY RHYMES, for Pianoforte and Voices—Cotsford Dick.

SINGING VERSES FOR CHILDREN—Lydia Coonley and others. New York, 1897.

SMALL SONGS FOR SMALL SINGERS—W. H. Neidlinger. (Coloured ill., Bobbett.) New York, Schirmer.

ST. NICHOLAS OPERETTAS. Century.

ST. NICHOLAS SONGS. Century.

SONGS OF CHILDHOOD—Eugene Field. Music by Reginald de Koven and others. New York, 1896.

STEVENSON SONG BOOK—Music by various composers. New York, 1897.

THREE OPERETTAS (THREE LITTLE KITTENS; SEVEN OLD LADIES OF LAVENDER TOWN; BOBBY SHAFTOE)—H. C. Bunner and Oscar Weil. New York, 1897.

Instrumental Music

HAYDN'S KINDER-SYMPHONIE—For Piano and Violin and Toy Instruments.

OUR FAVORITES (UNSERE LIEBLINGE). [Piano gems arranged by Carl Reinecke.] New York, Breitkopf and Hartel.

SCHUMANN, ROBERT—Album for Young Pianists. Op. 68.

Kinderball. (Dances, four hands, for Piano.) Op. 130.

Kinderscenen. (Piano.) Op. 15.

SCIENCE AND INVENTION

BAKER, RAY STANNARD—Boy's Book of Inventions. McClure, $2.00. [There is a second volume, $1.60.]

BALL, SIR ROBERT STAWELL—Starland. Ginn, $1.00.

DARWIN, CHARLES R.—What Mr. Darwin Saw in His Voyage Round the World in the Ship "Beagle." Harper, $3.00.

ILES, GEORGE—Flame, Electricity, and the Camera. Doubleday, $2.00 net.

MEADOWCROFT, W. H.—A B C of Electricity. Empire Publishing Co., $0.50.

NEWCOMB, SIMON—Astronomy for Everybody. McClure, $2.00 net.

SANTOS-DUMONT, ALBERTO—My Air-Ships. Century, $1.40 net.

SCIENTIFIC AMERICAN BOY: OR, THE CAMP AT WILLOW CLUMP ISLAND—A. Russell Bond. Munn and Co., $2.00.

SERVISS, GARRETT P.—Astronomy with an Opera Glass. Appleton, $1.50. [This book has been challenged.]

SLOANE, T. O'C.—Electric Toy-making.—Henley, $1.00. (*Vide* also St. John, T. M.—Three books on electricity. Scribner.)

TRAVEL

BOYESEN, H. H.—Boyhood in Norway. Scribner, $1.25.

The Modern Vikings. Scribner, $1.25.

BRASSEY, LADY A. (A.)—Around the World in the Yacht "Sunbeam." Holt, $2.00; Longmans (condensed), $0.75; Burt.

DU CHAILLU, P. B.—The Land of the Long Night. Scribner, $2.00.

Land of the Midnight Sun. Harper, 2 vols., $5.00.

JANVIER, THOMAS A.—The Aztec Treasure House. (Narrative.) Harper, $1.50.

JENKS, TUDOR—Boys' Book of Explorations. Doubleday, $2.00.

KENNAN, GEORGE—Tent Life in Siberia. Putnam, $0.50 to $1.25.

KNOX, THOMAS W.—Boy Travellers in Russia. Harper, $2.00.

Boy Travellers in South America. Harper. $2.00. [In these volumes there is a large amount of information which would have been more graphic, relieved of the artificial conversational style.]

LUMMIS, CHARLES F.—Some Strange Corners of Our Country. Century, $1.50.

NANSEN, FRIDTJOF—Farthest North: Record of a Voyage of the Ship "Fram." Harper, 2 vols., $4.00.

PEARY, MRS. J. D. AND M. A.—Children of the Arctic. Stokes, $1.20 net.

Snow Baby. Stokes, $1.20 net.

SLOCUM, JOSHUA—Sailing Alone Around the World in the Sloop "Spray." Whole edition, Century, $2.00; school edition, Scribner, $0.50.

STANLEY, HENRY M.—In Darkest Africa. Scribner, 2 vols., $7.50. [*Vide* also "My Dark Companions, and Their Strange Stories." Scribner, $2.00.]

TAYLOR, BAYARD—Boys of Other Countries. Putnam, $1.25.

FRENCH

"The collection of books which we call 'Bibliothèque Rose' (the paper bound edition has a pink cover; perhaps that is the reason why we call it Bibliothèque Rose) includes the most charming stories a child can wish for, especially those of Mme. de Ségur's and Zénaïde Fleuriot's. In this collection as well as in the Bibliothèque des Petits Enfants, and in the large illustrated albums, much will be found of interest to children of from six to ten years.

"For older boys and girls (10–15), I would recommend Bibliothèque des Mères de Famille. At the present time the only thing I remember about this collection is that there were in it a number of books translated from the German by Emmeline Raymond, and which used to give me much pleasure.

"As far as I can judge, girls and boys of this age enjoy Jules Verne,* Charles Wagner, H. Gréville, H. Malot, E. About, Erckmann-Chatrian,* Anatole France, Daudet, and La Fontaine, the two I have starred being special favourites with boys. Of course, I would not recommend for children everything by these authors. I have suggested many books in the Bibliothèque Rose; there are other writers in that collection, such, for example, as Mme. Cazin, Mlle. J. Gouraud, Maistre, Mayne-Reid, Mme. Pape-Carpantier, Mme. de Stolz, and Mme. de Witt,—all of whom have done some excellent juvenile work. But a parent should not be satisfied with a recommendation; personal judgment is the surest test.

"Regarding poetry, there are many short pieces by Mme. Tastu, well adapted for very young children. In the anthologies which are published you are most likely to find such pieces as Victor Hugo's 'L'enfant,' 'Pour les pauvres,' 'Après la bataille'; Lamartine's 'L'automne,' 'Milly'; extracts from Corneille and Racine; and Chateaubriand's well-known 'Combien j'ai douce souvenance.' Then there are a number of Coppée's poems; Béranger's 'Les souvenirs du peuple,' and 'A mon habit'; André Chénier's 'La jeune Captive'; Hégésippe Moreau's 'La Voulzie'; Brizeux's 'La pauvre fille'; Theuriet's 'La Chanson du Vannier'; and poems of Mme. Desborde-Valmore. This will give some idea of how rich the field of poetry is, which, with La Fontaine alone, would supply children with untold enjoyment.

"The educational value in most of the books which I have suggested consists chiefly in the attractive manner in which they are written; there is no 'leçon de morale' in disguise in the style, yet such books are more than well-written stories. Children read Mme. de Ségur's books with much more pleasure than they do the old-fashioned Berquin's, which are 'ennuyeux.' Such stories as Mme. de Ségur writes make a deep impression, since they teach agreeably to love the qualities which we grown-ups wish to see in children, and to dislike those faults which we would blame in them, even if, sometimes, the naughty child in the story *is* made attractive.

"You will see, we have no special books of animal stories, such as you publish in England and in America—unless you consider, of course, La Fontaine's fables, which do not give any practical knowledge of animal life. Books which appeal to the heart, or to the imagination, are very popular with French children, who are naturally sensitive and imaginative; but, after all, is it not so with every child, French or English or American?

"It has been my experience that American children (the very young ones), if they were able to read the French books French children of the same age read, enjoyed them quite as much. The difference in national temperament develops later on. The American boy or girl grows up more rapidly than the French boy or girl; acquires the practical sense sooner; has a more real view of life. Perhaps this is due largely to the fact that the French child has little independence, and hence is unpractical. But there is a compensation somewhere, for the French child's mind is subtler, and his imagination more vivid. I do not think we have any library system at present where children's work is a specialty; in fact, our public libraries are mostly frequented by grown-up people. I have never seen children, as far as I can recollect, in any of our libraries."—MLLE. EMILIE MICHEL, in a letter to the author.

Both Brentano and Dryrsen & Pfeiffer (successors to Christern), as well as W. R. Jenkins Co., New York, issue complete catalogues, French and German, in which illustrated books, magazines, and series of special volumes are suggested. They differ so markedly in prices, that no uniformity can be reached. But except in the case of illustrated albums, it may be claimed, generally, that the prices are reasonable.

ABOUT, EDMOND—Le Roi des Montagnes.

L'Homme à l'oreille Cassée.

CARRAUD, MME.—La petite Jeanne. Bibliothèque Rose.

DAUDET, ALPHONSE—Tartarin de Tarascon.

Tartarin sur les Alpes.

Lettres de Mon Moulin. (Contes.)

Le Petit Chose.

DEFOE—La Vie et les Aventures de Robinson Crusoé. Bibliothèque Rose. [*Vide* also in Bibl. des petits enfants, with "Gulliver's Travels."]

DOMBRE, ROGER—Tante Rabat Joie.

ERCKMANN-CHATRIAN—Le conscrit de 1813.

L'Ami Fritz.

FLEURIOT, MLLE. Z.—Le petit chef de famille. Bibliothèque Rose.

FLORIAN—Fables Illustrées par Vimar. Brentano, $2.70.

FRANCE, ANATOLE—Le Crime de Sylvestre Bonnard. [Crowned by the French Academy.]

Le Livre de Mon Ami. [For adults.]

GENLIS, MADAME DE—Bibliothèque Rose. Contes Moraux. *Vide* p. 66.

GRÉVILLE, HENRY (pseud. of Mme. Alice Durant)—Perdue. [*Vide* entire list.]

GRIMM—Contes Choisis. Bibliothèque Rose.

JOB—Le grand Napoléon des Petits Enfants. (Ill. coloured.) Brentano, $3.00.

LA FONTAINE—*Vide* Boutet de Monvel. Picture-Book section.

LA MOTTE-FOUQUE, BARON DE.—Undine and Sintram. [*Vide* English version. Houghton.]

MALOT, HECTOR—En famille.

Sans famille.

PERRAULT, CHARLES; MMES. D'AULNOY ET LE PRINCE DE BEAUMONT—Contes de Fées. Bibliothèque Rose. [*Vide* also Petite Bibliothèque Blanche, et ed. Perrault, ill. by many artists. Brentano, $2.70. *Vide* p. 36.]

PRESSENSÉ, MME. E. DE—La Maison Blanche et Histoire pour les écoliers. Bibliothèque Rose. [*Vide* also Bibl. des Petits Enfants.]

SANDEAU, JULES—La Maison de Penarvan.

SÉGUR, MME. DE—L'Auberge de l'Ange-Gardien. Bibliothèque Rose.

Un Bon Petit Diable.

Le Général Dourakine.

Mémoires d'un Ane.

Les Bons Enfants.

VERNE, JULES—Les Enfants du Capitaine Grant.

Cinq Semaines en Ballon.

Vingt Mille Lieues sous les Mers.

Le Tour du Monde en 80 Jours.

[All in the Bibliothèque Rose.]

WAGNER, CHARLES—Jeunesse.

Vaillance.

GERMAN

In the preparation of the following German list, the author begs to acknowledge in a general way his indebtedness to many sources. An authority on the subject is Wolgast, who is the author of "Vom Kinderbuch" (Leipzig, Teubner). One of the committee recommends the inclusion of all the stories by Johanna Spyri; another emphasises the importance of the work done by Ottilie Wildermuth, and appends the following interesting account in a letter: "'She was the wife of a professor in Tübingen, Swabia, and was born in 1817. She died in 1877. Long before she thought of writing for publication, she charmed a wide circle of friends and acquaintances with her talent for narrating the simple events, memories, and experiences of Swabian life. Most of her works must be considered, not as mere fiction, but as true pictures of the culture of that time, and as such will be of permanent value.' The same may be said of her children's books, although these are more fanciful and varied in their subject-matter, and appeal strongly to the imagination."

The Germans illustrate their A-B-C Bücher, their Nursery Rhymes, their Bilderbücher, and their Erzählungen in the most attractive fashion. Reference is particularly made to Herr Richter. Fairy Tales are read extensively by German children—and also by adults. Grimm, Hauff, Musäus, are about the best. Schmitt's Geschichten u. Erzählungen (of which there are perhaps from one to two hundred volumes) are excellent for boys and girls between ten and fifteen years. The Germans have paid such special attention to the selection and grading of juvenile literature, that their library lists are recommended to readers. The volumes here mentioned are not presented with any intention of making them definitive. Brentano will send, on application, "Verzeichnis einer Auswahl Vorzüglicher Bücher—Miniatur-Katalog.—Stilke, Berlin."

The reader is further referred to "Verzeichnis empfehlenswerter Jugendlektüre. Herausgegeben vom Wiener Volksbildungs-Verein, 1904."

ÄSOP—Fabeln. Mit 6 Buntbildern. Löwe.

AUS DEM LEBEN DER ZWERGE—Humorist. Bilderbuch.

BILDERBÜCHER. (Löwensohn.)

Der D-Zug Kommt. Eisenbahnbilderb. auf Papyrolin; auf Papier.

Für unsere A B C-Schützen.

Grimms Märchen.

Hänsel und Gretel.

Heerschau üb. d. Kriegsvölker Europas.

Hertwig, R., Eduard und Ferdinand. [*Vide* Catalogues.]

BILDERBÜCHER. (Scholz.)

LIEBE MÄRCHEN.

Dornröschen; Marienkind.

Aschenputtel; Rotkäppchen.

Hänsel und Gretel; Schneewittchen.

HEY-SPECKTER, W.—Fünfzig Fabeln f. Kinder. Jub.-Ausg.

Noch fünfzig Fabeln für Kinder. Jub.-Ausg.

Fabeln. 2 Bde. Schul-Ausgabe; 2 Bde. Feine Ausgabe.

THUMANN, P.—Für Mutter und Kind. Alte Reime mit neuen Bildern.

WIEDEMANN, F.—Hundert Geschichten für eine Mutter und ihre Kinder.

WILDERMUTH, O.—Aus der Kinderwelt.

ANDERS, H.—Gesammelte Märchen von Rübezahl.

ANDERSEN, H. C.—Sämtl. Märchen. Pr.-A. (Abel & Müller); V.-Ausg. (Abel & Müller); Pr.-Ausg. (Wartig).

Märchen. (Hendel); Löwe; Billige Ausgabe. (Weise.)

Ausgewählte Märchen. (Abel & Müller); Hrsg. v. Hamb. Jugendschr.-Ausschuss.

ARNDT, P.—Es war einmal. Märchen, Sagen u. Schwänke.

Im Märchenwalde.

Für brave Knaben.

Rübezahl. (Löwe); V.-Aug, (Löwe).

BECHSTEIN, L.—Märchenbuch. (Hendel).

BEEG, M.—Schulmädelgeschichten.

BEETZ, K. O.—Urd.; Deutsche Volksmärchen.

BLÜTHGEN, V.—Hesperiden. Märchen für jung und alt. Vollst. Ausg.

Lebensfrühling. Vier Erzählungen für Mädchen.

Der Märchenquell.

Der Weg zum Glück. Fünf Erzähl. f. Knaben.

CAMPE, J. H.—Robinson Krusoe von J. Hoffmann.

EMMY, TANTE—Märchen für grosse und kleine Kinder.

GRIMM, J. U. W.—Sämtl. Kinder- u. Hausmärchen. Mit Bildern v. L. Richter usw.

GUMPERT, TH. V.—Herzblättchens Zeitvertreib.

HAUFF, W.—Märchen. Ausw. f. d. Jugend. (Löwe).

HOFFMANN, FRZ.—Ausgew. Erzählungen. Bd. 1, 2, 3.

Das bunte Buch. Neue 150 moral. Erzählungen.

150 moralische Erzählungen.

Die Grossmutter.

Neuer deutscher Jugendfreund.

Märchen und Fabeln.

MÜLLER, K. A.—Rübezahl, der Herr des Riesengebirges.

MUSÄUS, J. K. A.—Märchen. Von K. A. Müller.

NIBELUNGENLIED—Für die Jugend, von A. Bacmeister.

OTTO, H.—Ilias, für die Jugend.

Nibelunge, für die Jugend. 2 Bdchn.

Sagen und Märchen für Achtjährige.

REICHENBACH—Buch der Tierwelt. Erzähl. u. Schildergn. a. d. Leben der Tiere. 2 Bde.

ROSEGGER, P.—Als ich noch der Waldbauernbub war. 3 Teile.

Waldferien.

SCHANZ, FR.—Heidefriedel.

Das Komtesschen und andere Erzählungen.

Rottraut u. Ilse.

Schulkindergeschichten.

Bunter Strauss. Märchen u. Erzählungen.

Unter der Tanne.

SCHANZ, P.—In der Pension u. anderes.

SCHOTT, CL.—Im Feenreich. Mit Bildern.

STEIN, A.—Mariens Tagebuch.

52 Sonntage.

Tagebuch dreier Kinder.

VILLAMARIA.—Elfenreigen. Nordische Märchen.

WILDERMUTH, O.—Aus Nord und Süd.

Aus Schloss und Hütte.

Jugendschriften. V.-A.; Inhalt s. Abt. Schriften für die reifere weibl. Jugend.

Kindergruss.

CERVANTES—Don Quichote. Für d. Jugend v. Frz. Hoffmann; für Schule und Haus bearbeitet von Höller. (Schaffstein). Illustriert; Für die Jugend von P. Moritz. V.-Ausg.; (Weise).

COOPER, J. F.—Conanchet. Von Frz. Hoffmann.

Der rote Freibeuter. Von P. O. Höcker. (Löwe).

Lederstrumpf-Erzählgn. F. d. Jugend v. Kl. Bernhard; Für die Jugend v. O. Höcker. (Löwe); v. Frz. Hoffmann; v. Fr. Meister. Pr.-A.; Einzeln: Der Wildtöter; Der letzte der Mohikaner; Der Pfadfinder; Lederstrumpf; Der alte Trapper; v. P. Moritz. Gesamt-Ausg.; Einzeln: Der letzte Mohikaner; Der Pfadfinder; Lederstrumpf od. die Ansiedler; Der Wildsteller od. die Prärie; Der Wildtöter.

Die Prärie. Für die Jugend. (Weise.)

Der Spion. Für die Jugend von E. Bensler.

DAHN, F. U. TH.—Walhall. Germanische Götter-u. Heldensagen. Ausgabe mit Bildern.

HAUFF, W.—Lichtenstein. Für die Jugend. (Weise.)

LILIENCRON, D. V.—Gedichte. Auswahl für die Jugend.

EBNER-ESCHENBACH, M. V.—Die arme Kleine.

GUMPERT, TH. V.—Töchter-Album.

HARTNER, E. (E. E. H. v. Twardowska.)—Pension und Elternhaus.

HEINZ, T. V. (Henny von Tempelhoff.)—Goldköpfchen.

Pension Velden.

Tante Sybille.

HELDERN, T. (Toni Lindner.)—Die Backfischpension.

RHODEN, E. V. (Emma Friedrich-Friedrich.)—Der Trotzkopf. Mit Bildern; Billige Ausgabe.

Trotzkopfs Brautzeit. Mit Bildern; Billige Ausgabe.

(Wildhagen), Aus Trotzkopfs Ehe. Mit Bildern; Billige Ausgabe.

(S. la Chapelle-Roobol), Trotzkopf als Grossmutter.

Der Trotzkopf. 3 Bde. Feine Ausg. in hell. Damastlnw. geb., in eleg. Hülse.

ROSEGGER, P.—Ernst u. heiter. Volksausg. f. Österreich.

SCHMIDT, H.—In Backfischchens Kaffeekränzchen.

WILDERMUTH, O.—Jugendschriften. Volks-Ausg. 22 Bde.

1. Ein einsam Kind. Die Wasser im Jahre 1824; 2. Drei Schulkameraden. Der Spiegel der Zwerglein; 3. Eine seltsame Schule. Bärbeles Weihnachten; 4. Eine Königin. Der Kinder Gebet; 5. Spätes Glück. Die drei Schwestern vom Walde; 6. Die Ferien auf Schloss Bärensprung. Der Sandbub oder Wer hat's am besten?; 7. Cherubino u. Zephirine. Kann sein, 's ist auch so recht; 8. Brüderchen und Schwesterchen. Der Einsiedler im Walde; 9. Der Peterli von Emmenthal. Zwei Märchen für die Kleinsten; 10. Krieg und Frieden. Emmas Pilgerfahrt; 11. Das braune Lenchen. Des Königs Patenkind; 12. Nach Regen Sonnenschein. Frau Luna. Das Bäumlein im Walde; 13. Die Nachbarskinder. Kordulas erste Reise. Balthasars Apfelbäume; 14. Die wunderbare Höhle. Das Steinkreuz. Unsere alte Marie; 15. Der kluge Bruno. Eine alte Schuld. Heb' auf, was Gott dir vor die Türe legt; 16. Elisabeth. Die drei Christbäume. Klärchens Genesung. Das Feental; 17. Vom armen Unstern; 18. Es ging ein Engel durch das Haus. Des Herrn Pfarrers Kuh. Die erste Seefahrt; 19. Schwarze Treue; 20. Das Osterlied. Die Kinder der Heide; 21. Hinauf und Hinab; 22. Der rote Hof.

NATURE

ARNOLD, A. F.—The Sea-Beach at Ebb-Tide. Century, $2.40 net.

BOSTOCK, F. C.—The Training of Wild Animals. Century, $1.00 net.

BURROUGHS, JOHN—Squirrels and Other Fur-Bearers. (Ill. after Audubon.) Houghton, $1.00.

Wake Robin. Houghton, $1.00 net.

CHAPMAN, FRANK R.—Bird-Life: A Guide to the Study of Our Common Birds. (Ill., Seton.) Appleton, $2.00.

DOUBLEDAY, MRS. F. N. (pseud., Neltje Blanchan)—Bird Neighbors. Doubleday, $2.00. [American and local. *Vide* same author's "Birds that Hunt and Are Hunted," $2.00.]

Nature's Garden. Doubleday, $3.00 net.

DUGMORE, A. RADCLYFFE—Nature and the Camera. Doubleday, $1.35 net.

GIBSON, W. H.—Blossom Hosts and Insect Guests. Newson, $0.80.

Eye Spy. Harper, $2.50.

Sharp Eyes. Harper, $2.50.

HOLLAND, W. J.—Butterfly Book. Doubleday, $3.00 net. [*Vide* same author's "Moth Book," $4.00 net.]

HORNADAY, WILLIAM T.—American Natural History. Scribner, $3.50 net. [*Vide* same author's "Two Years in a Jungle," $2.50.]

KEELER, HARRIET L.—Our Native Trees and How to Identify Them. Scribner, $2.00 net. [*Vide* also the "Tree Book." Julia E. Rogers. Doubleday, $4.00 net.]

MILLER, OLIVE THORNE—The First Book of Birds. Houghton, $1.00. [There is a second book.]

MORLEY, MARGARET W.—The Bee People. McClurg, $1.25.

PARSONS, FRANCES THEODORA (formerly Mrs. Dana)—How to Know Wild Flowers. Scribner, $2.00 net. [*Vide* also same author's "According to the Seasons." Scribner, $1.75 net.]

SETON, ERNEST THOMPSON—Biography of a Grizzly. Century, $1.50.

Wild Animals I have Known. Scribner, $2.00. [*Vide* also same author's "Lives of the Hunted."]

SHALER, NATHANIEL S.—Story of the Continent. Ginn, $0.75.

First Book in Geology. Heath, $0.60.

SHARP, DALLAS L.—Wild Life Near Home. Century, $2.00. [*Vide* also same author's "A Watcher in the Woods." Century, $0.84.]

THOREAU, HENRY D.—Walden. Houghton, $1.50 to $3.00.

TORREY, BRADFORD—Every-day Birds. (Ill. after Thoreau.) Houghton, $1.00.

WRIGHT, MABEL OSGOOD—Citizen Bird. Macmillan, $1.50 net.

BIOGRAPHY

ABBOTT, J. S. C.—Daniel Boone, and the Early Settlement of Kentucky. Dodd, $0.75.

David Crockett and Early Texan History. Dodd, $0.75.

Kit Carson, the Pioneer of the Far West. Dodd, $0.75.

ALCOTT, LOUISA MAY—Life, Letters, and Journals. (Ed., E. D. Cheney.) Little, Brown, $1.50.

BARNES, JAMES—Midshipman Farragut. Appleton, $1.00.

BOLTON, MRS. S. K.—Poor Boys Who Became Famous. Crowell, $1.50. [This author has written many books of a similar character for boys and girls.]

BROOKS, E. S.—Historic Boys. Putnam, $1.25.

Historic Girls. Putnam, $1.25. [Same author wrote "Historic Dwarfs" for *St. Nicholas Magazine*. His facts have been challenged.]

Chivalric Days. Putnam, $1.25.

BUTTERWORTH, HEZEKIAH—The Boys of Greenway Court. [The Early Days of Washington. Many librarians would challenge this.] Appleton, $1.50.

FRANKLIN, BENJAMIN—Autobiography. Houghton, $0.75.

GARLAND, HAMLIN—Ulysses S. Grant. McClure, $2.50.

JOAN OF ARC—*Vide* Boutet de Monvel. [Picture-book section.]

KELLER, HELEN—The Story of My Life. Doubleday, $1.50 net.

LEE, ROBERT E.—*Vide* Beacon Biographies. Trent, W. P. [The Lives of Lee, J. E. B. Stuart, and Stonewall Jackson have yet to be treated satisfactorily for young people.]

NICOLAY, HELEN—Boys' Life of Lincoln. Century, $1.50.

OBER, FREDERICK A.—Columbus; Pizarro; DeSoto. Harper, $1.00 net each. [This author's style is picturesque.]

RIIS, JACOB A.—The Making of an American: An Autobiography. Macmillan, $1.50 net.

SCUDDER, HORACE E.—George Washington. Houghton, $0.75. [*Vide* also E. E. Hale's "Life of Washington." Putnam, $1.75.]

SEAWELL, M. E.—Decatur and Somers. Appleton, $1.00.

Twelve Naval Captains. Scribner, $1.25.

Paul Jones. Appleton, $1.00.

SEELYE, ELIZABETH E.—The Story of Columbus. Appleton, $1.75.

SOUTHEY, ROBERT—Life of Nelson. [*Vide* ed., Macmillan, Warne, Crowell, Dutton, Lothrop, etc.]

WISTER, OWEN—U. S. Grant. (Beacon Biography.) Small, $0.75 net. [This is the same series as referred to under Lee, in which Norman Hapgood has written on Daniel Webster.]

HISTORY

ALTON, E. (pseud, of Edmund Bailey)—Among the Law Makers. Scribner, $1.50.

BARNES, JAMES—Yankee Ships and Yankee Sailors. Macmillan, $1.50.

CALLCOTT, M. (D.)—Little Arthur's History of England. Crowell, $0.60.

Little Arthur's History of France. Crowell, $0.60. [Both volumes have a certain value in the history of children's books.]

COFFIN, C. C.—Boys of '76. Harper, $2.00. [Same author wrote "Boys of '61." Estes, $2.00.]

CREASY, E. S.—Fifteen Decisive Battles of the World. Harper, $1.00.

DICKENS, CHARLES—Child's History of England. Houghton, $1.00 to $2.50.

DOLE, C. F.—The Young Citizen. Heath, $0.45.

EGGLESTON, E. and SEELYE (MRS.), E. E.—Brant and Red Jacket. Dodd, $0.75.

FISKE, JOHN—He has written a United States History. (Houghton.) His larger contributions on periods are so excellent in their narrative style as to recommend themselves for young readers of high-school age. [*Vide* also Edward Eggleston's "Household History of the United States." Appleton, $2.50.]

GRIFFIS, W. E.—Brave Little Holland and What She Taught Us. Houghton, $1.25.

GREENWOOD, GRACE—Merrie England; Bonnie Scotland. [Out of print, but re-publication strongly advised by librarians. Miss Burnite, of the Cleveland Public Library, recently edited the "Ballads Retold." Ginn, $0.50.]

Stories and Legends; Stories and Sights of France and Italy. [Also out of print.]

HAWTHORNE, NATHANIEL—Grandfather's Chair. Containing also Biographical Stories. Houghton, $1.25.

JENKS, TUDOR—Our Army for Our Boys. (Ill. Ogden.) Moffat, Yard, $2.00 net. [Mr. Jenks is also the author of the lives of John Smith and Miles

Standish (Century); of a series of historical and social studies for children, the first volume called "When America Was New" (Crowell.); and of another series, Lives of Great Writers (Barnes.).]

KIEFFER, H. M.—Recollections of a Drummer Boy. (A Civil War biographical story.) Houghton, $1.50.

MARSHALL, HELEN—An Island Story. [A history of England, written by an Australian. The book is in sumptuous *format*.] Stokes, $2.50 net.

MCDOUGALL, ISABEL—Little Royalties. Revell, $1.25.

PARKMAN, FRANCIS—The Oregon Trail. (Ill., Remington.) Little, Brown, $4.00; $2.00.

The Conspiracy of Pontiac. (2 vols.) Little, Brown, $3.00.

ROOSEVELT, THEODORE, AND LODGE, HENRY CABOT—Hero Tales from American History. Century, $1.50.

SCOTT, SIR WALTER—Tales of a Grandfather. Macmillan, $2.00.

STOCKTON, FRANK R.—Buccaneers and Pirates of our Coast. Macmillan, $1.50.

TARBELL, IDA M.—He Knew Lincoln. McClure, $0.50 net.

YONGE, CHARLOTTE M.—Young Folk's History of England. Lothrop, $1.50. [*Vide* Miss Yonge's "Book of Golden Deeds." Macmillan, $1.00.]

HISTORICAL STORIES

AGUILAR, GRACE—The Days of Bruce. Appleton, $1.00. [She also wrote "A Mother's Recompense" and "Home Influence."]

ANDREWS, MARY RAYMOND SHIPMAN—The Perfect Tribute. (A Story of Lincoln.) Scribner, $0.50.

BARNES, JAMES—For King or Country. Harper, $1.50.

BENNETT, JOHN—Master Skylark. (A Story of Shakespeare's Time.) Century, $1.50.

Barnaby Lee. Century, $1.50.

BULWER-LYTTON, EDWARD—Harold, the Last of the Saxons. (2 vols.) Little, Brown, $1.25 each.

Last Days of Pompeii. Little, Brown, $1.25.

Last of the Barons. (A Story of the Earl of Warwick.) [2 vols.] Little, Brown, $1.25 each.

DAVIS, M. E. M.—In War Times at La Rose Blanche. Lothrop, $1.25.

DOYLE, A. CONAN—White Company. (A 14th-century story.) Harper, $1.75.

Micah Clarke. (A 17th-century story.) Harper, $1.75.

EGGLESTON, GEORGE CARY—Signal Boys. Putnam, $1.25.

Southern Soldier Stories. Macmillan, $1.50.

Strange Stories from History. Harper, $0.60.

HALE, EDWARD E.—A Man Without a Country. Little, Brown, $0.50 to $1.25.

HENTY, G. A.—Lion of the North. (A Tale of Gustavus Adolphus.) Scribner, $1.50.

St. George for England. (A Tale of Cressy and Poitiers.) Scribner, $1.50.

With Clive in India. Scribner, $1.50.

With Wolfe in Canada. Scribner, $1.50. [When one is read, the formula for all is discovered.]

KEARY, ANNIE—A York and Lancaster Rose. Macmillan, $1.00.

KINGSLEY, CHARLES—Westward Ho! Macmillan, $0.50 to $2.00. [This book, a tale of the 16th century, was recently debarred from one of the library centres in England.]

KNAPP, ADELINE—The Boy and the Baron. (Germany of feudal times.) Century, $1.00.

MARSHALL, BEATRICE—The Siege of York. (In the days of Thomas, Lord Fairfax.) Dutton, $1.50. [For older girls.]

MATTHEWS, BRANDER—Tom Paulding. (A story of New York and a treasure.) Century, $1.50.

PAGE, THOMAS NELSON—Two Little Confederates. Scribner, $1.50.

Among the Camps. Scribner, $1.50.

PORTER, JANE—The Scottish Chiefs. Dutton, $2.50. (Ill., T. H. Robinson. A Story of William Wallace. Miss Aguilar's book, "In the Days of Bruce," is considered a sequel.)

Thaddeus of Warsaw. [Various editions: Coates, Burt, Routledge, Warne.]

PYLE, HOWARD—Men of Iron. (A 14th-century story.) Harper, $2.00.

SCOTT, SIR WALTER—Ivanhoe. Macmillan, $1.25.

The Talisman. Macmillan, $1.25.

Quentin Durward. Macmillan, $1.25.

Rob Roy. Macmillan, $1.25. [As an introduction, these should lead the way to others.]

SEAWELL, M. E.—Little Jarvis. Appleton, $1.00.

STOWE, HARRIET B.—Uncle Tom's Cabin. Houghton, $1.00. (Ill., Kemble, $4.00.) [This is reluctantly included; many are strongly in favor of keeping from children such partisan writing; the cause for sectional feeling has been removed to an extent.]

TOMLINSON, E. T.—Boy Officers of 1812. Lothrop, Lee, $1.25.

Search for Andrew Field. Lothrop, Lee, $1.25.

TWAIN, MARK (pseud, of Samuel L. Clemens)—The Prince and the Pauper. (16th century.) Harper, $1.75.

WALLACE, LEW—Ben Hur. (A Tale of the Christ.) Harper, $1.50 to $10.00.

YONGE, CHARLOTTE M.—The Lances of Lynwood, Lothrop, Lee, $1.00. [Miss Yonge on children's reading is seen to great advantage.]

INDIAN STORIES

BAYLOR, FRANCES C. (Mrs. F. C. [B.] Belger.)—Juan and Juanita. Houghton, $1.50.

BROOKS, NOAH—The Boy Emigrants. Scribner, $1.25.

The Boy Settlers. (Early times in Kansas.) Scribner, $1.25.

CATHERWOOD, MARY HARTWELL—Heroes of the Middle West. Ginn, $0.50.

COOPER, JAMES FENIMORE—Deerslayer. Houghton, $1.00.

The Spy. Houghton, $1.00; Appleton, $1.50. [The entire Leatherstocking series should be read.]

The Last of the Mohicans. Houghton, $1.00.

CUSTER, MRS. E. B.—Boots and Saddles. Harper, $1.50. [An account of life in camp out West, and of her husband's career. Campaigns against the Indians are described. A second book is called "Tenting on the Plains." Harper, $1.50.]

DEMING, E. W.—Little Indian-Folk. Stokes, $1.25.

Little Red People. Stokes, $1.25. [*Vide* the same author's "Indian Child Life." Stokes, $2.00.]

DRAKE, F. S.—Indian History for Young Folks. Harper, $3.00.

EASTMAN, CHARLES A.—Indian Boyhood. McClure, $1.60 net.

MUNROE, KIRK—The Flamingo Feather. (A tale of Huguenots and Spaniards.) Harper, $0.60.

STODDARD, W. O.—Little Smoke. (A tale of the Sioux.) Appleton, $1.50.

Red Mustang. Harper, $0.60.

Two Arrows. Harper, $0.60.

STORIES

ABBOT, ALICE BALCH—A Frigate's Namesake. Century, $1.00.

ALCOTT, LOUISA MAY—Eight Cousins. Little, Brown, $1.50.

Little Women. *Ibid.*

Little Men. *Ibid.*

Old Fashioned Girl. *Ibid.*

ALDEN, W. L.—Cruise of the Canoe Club. Harper, $0.60.

ANDREWS, JANE—The Seven Little Sisters who Lived on the Round Ball That Floats in the Air. Lothrop, Lee, $1.00.

Ten Boys who Lived on the Road from Long Ago to Now. Lothrop, Lee, $1.00.

BARBOUR, RALPH—The Crimson Sweater. Century, $1.50. [The same author wrote "Captain of the Crew"; "For the Honor of the School."]

BARRIE, JAMES M.—Peter Pan. (Ill., Arthur Rackham.) Scribner, $5.00.

BLACKMORE, R. D.—Lorna Doone. [For older readers.] Harper, $2.00.

BURNETT, F. H.—Little Lord Fauntleroy. Scribner, $1.25.

The Little Princess. [An enlarged "Sara Crew."] Scribner, $2.00.

CHAMPNEY, E. W.—Howling Wolf. Lothrop, $1.25.

Pierre and his Poodle. Dodd, $1.00.

Paddy O'Leary and his Learned Pig. Dodd, $1.00.

COOLIDGE, SUSAN (pseud., S. C. Woolsey.)—Eyebright. Little, Brown, $1.25.

DANA, RICHARD H., JR.—Two Years Before the Mast. Houghton, $1.00.

DE AMICIS, EDMONDO—Cuore: an Italian Schoolboy's Journal. Crowell, $1.00.

DEFOE, DANIEL—Robinson Crusoe. (Ill., Rheid Brothers.) Russell, Harper, $1.50.

DICKENS, CHARLES—David Copperfield. Houghton, 2 vols., $3.00.

Tale of Two Cities. Houghton, $1.50. [*Vide* also "Christmas Carol." These should encourage the children to follow up one work with another.]

DODGE, MARY MAPES—Donald and Dorothy. Century, $1.50. [*Vide* her "Baby-Days."]

Hans Brinker, or the Silver Skates. (New Amsterdam edition.) Scribner, $1.50.

DUNCAN, NORMAN—Adventures of Billy Topsail. Revell, $1.50. [This is a good example of an adventurous story, well told.]

EDGEWORTH, MARIA—Waste Not, Want Not. Heath, $0.20.

Popular Tales. Macmillan, $1.50.

Tales. (Ed., Austin Dobson.) Stokes, $1.50.

Early Lessons. Routledge, $1.00. [The Macmillans also publish "Moral Tales," $1.00; Routledge, "Parent's Assistant," $1.00.]

EGGLESTON, GEORGE CARY—Big Brother. Putnam, $1.25.

Captain Sam. Putnam, $1.25.

EWING, MRS. J. H.—Jackanapes. Little, Brown, $0.50; Crowell, $0.60.

Story of a Short Life. Dutton, $1.00; Crowell, $0.75.

Timothy Shoes. [Short story.]

The Brownies. Young, $1.00; Burt, $0.75.

FAIRSTAR, MRS. (pseud. of Richard Hengist Horne).—Memoirs of a London Doll. Brentano, $1.25.

FLETCHER, R. H.—Marjory and Her Papa. Century, $1.00.

FRENCH, ALLEN—The Junior Cup. Century, $1.50. [*Vide* the same author's excellent legendary-historical tale, "Sir Marrok." Century, $1.00.]

GASKELL, E. C. (S.)—Cranford. (For older readers.) Macmillan, $1.50.

GATES, ELEANOR (Mrs. Richard Walton Tully.)—Biography of a Prairie Girl. Century, $1.50.

GILSON, ROY ROLFE—Katrina. (For older readers.) Baker and Taylor, $1.50.

GOLDSMITH, OLIVER—The Vicar of Wakefield. [Ill., Hugh Thomson. *Vide* also Caldecott.] Macmillan, $1.50.

Goody Two Shoes. (Ed., Welsh.) Heath, $0.20. [*Vide* also edition, Macmillan.]

GOULDING, FRANK—The Young Marooners. Dodd. No price stated. [There is a companion volume, "Marooner's Island." This Southern writer is little known.]

HALE, LUCRETIA P.—The Peterkin Papers. Houghton, $1.50. [There is another volume, "The Last of the Peterkins, with Others of Their Kin."]

HARKER, L. ALLEN—Concerning Paul and Fiametta. Scribner, $1.25. [This book is delightfully human; some would consider it more a story *about* children than *for* children.]

HIGGINSON, THOMAS W.—Tales of the Enchanted Islands of the Atlantic. Macmillan, $1.50.

HILL, C. T.—Fighting a Fire. [Stories of real life.] Century, $1.50.

HUGHES, RUPERT—The Lakerim Athletic Club. Century, $1.50.

The Dozen from Lakerim. Century, $1.50.

HUGHES, THOMAS—Tom Brown's School Days at Rugby. Macmillan, $1.50; Houghton, $1.00. [For older readers, there is "Tom Brown at Oxford."]

IRVING, WASHINGTON—Bracebridge Hall. (Ill., Caldecott.) Macmillan, $1.50.

Old Christmas. (Ill., Caldecott.) Macmillan, $1.50.

JACKSON, HELEN HUNT—Ramona. Little, Brown, $1.50.

Nelly's Silver Mine. (A Story of Colorado life.) Little, Brown, $1.50.

Cat Stories. Little, Brown, $2.00.

JAMISON, MRS. C. V.—Lady Jane. Century, $1.50.

Toinette's Philip. Century, $1.50. [Descriptions of early New-Orleans life.]

JEWETT, SARAH ORNE—Betty Leicester. Houghton, $1.25.

JOHNSON, ROSSITER—Phaeton Rogers. Scribner, $1.50.

KING, CAPT. CHARLES—Cadet Days. Harper, $1.25.

KIPLING, RUDYARD—"Captains Courageous." (A tale of the Gloucester fishermen.) Century, $1.50.

LAMB, CHARLES AND MARY—Mrs. Leicester's School. Dent (ill., Winifred Green, in Kate Greenaway style). Macmillan, $2.25.

LA RAMÉE, LOUISE DE (Ouida)—Dog of Flanders. Lippincott, $1.50.

LUCAS, E. V. (ED.)—Old-Fashioned Tales. Stokes, $1.50.

(ED.) Forgotten Tales of Long Ago. Stokes, $1.50.

MARRYATT, FREDERICK—Masterman Ready. Macmillan, $1.50; Routledge, $1.25. [Some librarians would reject Marryatt as they would Ballentyne; others would include him as they would Ballentyne.]

MARTINEAU, HARRIET—The Crofton Boys. Routledge, $0.75; Heath, $0.30.

MATHEWS, MARGARET H.—Dr. Gilbert's Daughters. Coates, $0.75.

MOFFETT, CLEVELAND—Careers of Danger and Daring. [Stories of real life.] Century, $1.50.

MOLESWORTH, MRS.—Two Little Waifs. Macmillan, $1.00.

Carrots. Macmillan, $1.50; Crowell, $0.75.

MUNROE, KIRK—Cab and Caboose. Tale published in *St. Nicholas*.

Derrick Sterling. Harper, $0.60.

MYRTLE, HARRIET—Country Scenes.

Man of Snow. [Out of print, but re-publication strongly advised by librarians.]

OLLIVANT, ALFRED—Bob, Son of Battle. Doubleday, $1.50. [Strongly recommended for its vigour and its vividness.]

OTIS, JAMES (pseud, of J. O. Kaler)—Toby Tyler; or, Ten Weeks with a Circus. Harper, $0.60.

Mr. Stubbs's Brother. Harper, $0.60.

PAULL, MRS. H. B.—Only a Cat. Whitaker, $1.25. [An excellent story.]

PIER, ARTHUR S.—Boys of St. Timothy's. Houghton, $1.50.

PYLE, HOWARD—Jack Ballister's Fortunes. Century, $2.00.

RICHARDS, LAURA E.—Captain January. Estes, $0.50.

SANDFORD, MRS. D. P.—The Little Brown House and the Children who Lived in It. Dutton, $2.00.

SAUNDERS, MARSHALL Beautiful Joe. Am. Bap., $0.25.

SCUDDER, HORACE E.—Bodley Books. Houghton, 8 vols., $12.00 set; $1.50 each.

The Children's Book. (Edited.) Houghton, $2.50.

SÉGUR, MME. S. (R.) DE—The Story of a Donkey. Heath, $0.20.

SEWELL, ANNA—Black Beauty. Page, $1.25.

SHARP, EVELYN—The Youngest Girl in School. Macmillan, $1.50.

SHERWOOD, M. M. (B.)—The Fairchild Family. Stokes, $1.50. [Recommended for historic value.]

SHAW, F. L.—Castle Blair. Little, Brown, $1.00.

SPYRI, J.—Story of Heidi. DeWolfe Fiske, $1.50; Ginn, $0.40.

STEVENSON, ROBERT LOUIS—Treasure Island. Scribner, $1.00. ["Kidnapped" is a sequel.]

Black Arrow. Scribner, $1.00. [A good "penny-dreadful."]

STOCKTON, FRANK R.—A Jolly Fellowship. Scribner, $1.50.

STUART, RUTH MCENERY—The Story of Babette. Harper, $1.50. [*Vide* the same author's "Solomon Crow's Christmas Pocket." Harper, $1.25.]

TAGGART, MARION AMES—The Little Gray House. McClure, $1.25. [The author has unfortunately been persuaded to continue her story in a second volume.]

TRIMMER, SARAH K.—History of the Robins. Heath, $0.25. [Historic interest.]

TROWBRIDGE, JOHN T.—The Tinkham Brothers' Tide-Mill. Lothrop, Lee, $1.25.

His Own Master. Lothrop, Lee, $1.25.

Jack Hazard and His Fortunes. Coates, $1.25. (In a series.)

TWAIN, MARK (pseud. of Samuel L. Clemens.)—Huckleberry Finn. Harper, $1.75.

Tom Sawyer. Harper, $1.75.

VAN DYKE, HENRY—The First Christmas Tree. (Ill., Pyle.) Scribner, $1.50.

The Story of the Other Wise Man. Harper, $1.00.

VERNE, JULES—A Tour of the World in Eighty Days. [*Vide* various editions.]

Twenty Thousand leagues under the Sea. Coates, $0.75. [*Vide* various editions.]

WIGGIN, KATE DOUGLAS—Half a Dozen House Keepers. Altemus, $0.75.

Rebecca of Sunnybrook Farm. Houghton, $1.25.

The Bird's Christmas Carol. Houghton, $0.50.

Timothy's Quest. (Ill., Oliver Herford.) Houghton, $1.50.

Polly Oliver's Problem. Houghton, $1.00.

WYSS, J. R. V. AND MONTOLIEU, BARONNE DE—Swiss Family Robinson. Warne, $2.50; Dutton, $2.50. [Cheaper editions.]

BOOKS ABOUT CHILDREN

ALDRICH, THOMAS BAILEY—Story of a Bad Boy. (Ill., Frost.) Houghton, $2.00; $1.25.

EGGLESTON, EDWARD—The Hoosier School-Boy. Scribner, $1.00.

EWALD, CARL (Tr., DeMattos.)—My Little Boy. Scribner, $1.00.

GILSON, ROY ROLFE—Mother and Father. Harper, $1.25.

HOWELLS, WILLIAM DEAN—A Boy's Town. (Told for *Harper's Young People.*) Harper, $1.25.

HUTTON, LAURENCE—A Boy I knew and Four Dogs. Harper, $1.25.

LARCOM, LUCY—New England Girlhood. Houghton, $0.75. [*Vide* various editions.]

MARTIN, EDWARD S.—The Luxury of Children. Harper, $1.75 net.

RICHARDS, LAURA E.—When I Was Your Age. Estes, $1.25.

WARNER, CHARLES DUDLEY—Being a Boy. Houghton, $1.25.

WHITTIER, JOHN G. (ED.)—Child-Life in Prose. Houghton, $2.00.

ETHICS AND RELIGION

BIBLE FOR YOUNG PEOPLE (Ed., Mrs. Joseph Gilder; Bishop Potter.)—Century, $1.50; ed. de luxe, $3.00.

BUNYAN, JOHN—Pilgrim's Progress. Century (Ill., Brothers Rhead.), $1.50; Scribner (Ill., Byam Shaw), $2.50 net.

FIELD, EUGENE—A Little Book of Profitable Tales. Scribner, $1.25.

GATTY, MRS.—Parables from Nature. Bell (2 vols.); Macmillan, $1.50; Dutton (Everyman's Library.).

HOUGHTON, LOUISE SEYMOUR—Telling Bible Stories. Scribner, $1.25. [R. G. Moulton has edited for Macmillan a Children's Series of Bible Stories.]

PSALMS OF DAVID (Ill., Brothers Rhead.)—Revell, $2.50.

RUSKIN, JOHN—Sesame and Lilies. [*Vide* editions, McClurg, Mosher, Crowell, etc.]

III. BIBLIOGRAPHICAL NOTE

A few references of a miscellaneous character are here given:

BIBLE in Elementary Schools (J. G. Fitch)—*Nineteenth Century*, 36:817.

BOOK, The Child and His (Mrs. E. M. Field)—London, Wells, Gardner, Darton & Co., 1891.

BOOK, The Child and the (Gerald Stanley Lee)—Putnam, 1907.

BOOK-PLATES, Modern, and their Designers (Gleeson White)—*The Studio*, 1898–99, Supplement 1.

BOOKS, Better, Some Means by Which Children May Be Led to Read (Clara W. Hunt)—*Library Journal*, 24:147.

BOOKS, Children's (Caroline M. Hewins)—*Public Library*, 1:190.

BOOKS, Children's, and Children (H. A. Page)—*Contemporary*, 11:7.

BOOKS for Boys and Girls, On Some (From *Blackwood*)—*Liv. Age*, 209:3.

BOOKS for Children, Illustrated (W. M. Thackeray)—*Fraser*, 33:495 (1846).

BOOKS for Children That Have Lived (C. Welsh)—*Library* [London], n.s., 1:314.

BOOKS, The Best Hundred, for Children—*Liv. Age*, 225:132.

CARNEGIE Libraries, Giving (I. F. Marcosson)—*World's Work*, 9:6092.

CULTURE, On a Possible Popular (T. Wright)—*Contemporary*, 40:25.

ENGLISH, On the Teaching of (Percival Chubb)—Macmillan, 1902.

GIRL, The Reading of the Modern (Florence B. Low)—*Nineteenth Century*, 59:278.

GIRLS Read, What (E. G. Salmon)—*Nineteenth Century*, 20:515.

HENTY Book, What You Can Get Out of a (Caroline M. Hewins)—*Wisconsin Library Bulletin*, Sept.-Oct., 1906.

LESSON-BOOKS, Our Ancestor's (S. E. Braine)—*Liv. Age*, 222:522.

LIBRARIANA: An Outline of the Literature of Libraries (F. J. Teggart)—*Library Journal*, 25:223, 577, 625.

LIBRARIES, Home, for Poor Children (Frances J. Olcott)—*Chautauquan*, 39:374.

LIBRARIES, Public, in the United States: Their History, Condition, and Management. Bureau of Education, 1876.

LIBRARIES, Small, Hints to (M. W. Plummer)—Pratt Institute, 1902.

LIBRARIES, The Free Travelling, in Wisconsin. The Story of Their Growth, etc. *Wisconsin Free Library Commission*, Madison, 1897. [Interesting monograph.]

LIBRARIES, What Free, are doing for Children (Mary W. Plummer.)—*Library Journal*, *Vide* vol. 22.

LIBRARY, The Free: Its History, etc. (John J. Ogle)—London, Allen, 1897.

LIBRARY Literature in England and in the United States During the Nineteenth Century (F. J. Teggart)—*Library Journal*, 26:257.

LIBRARY Movement in the South Since 1899 (Anne Wallace)—*Library Journal*, 32:253.

LIBRARY Work with Children (Arabella H. Jackson)—Carnegie Library, Pittsburgh, Pa. [Statistical.]

LIBRARY Work, Rational, With Children, and the Preparation For It (Frances J. Olcott)—Carnegie Library, Pittsburgh. Boston: A. L. A. Pub. Board. Reprint Series, No. 9, $0.05.

LISTS, Reading, Fallacies of—*Liv. Age*, 170:218.

LITERATURE, Cheap (Helen Bosanquet)—*Contemporary*, 79:671.

LITERATURE, Cheap, for Village Children—*Liv. Age*, 138:296.

LITERATURE, Children's (Ellen M. Henrotin)—*National Magazine* (Boston), 7:373.

LITERATURE for the Little Ones (E. G. Salmon)—*Nineteenth Century*, 22:563.

LITERATURE, Modern, Children and (H. Sutton)—*Liv. Age*, 192:287.

MUSIC, Public School (S. W. Cole)—*New Eng. Mag.*, n.s., 13:328.

MUSIC in Schools, Teaching of (J. C. Hadden)—*Nineteenth Century*, 42:142.

MUSIC, The Introduction of the Study of, into the Public Schools of Boston and of America (J. C. Johnson)—*Boston*, 1:622.

NOVELS, Some, to Read (Caroline M. Hewins)—*Traveller's Record*, Feb.-Mar., 1889.

PERIODICALS, Children's Books and (Abby L. Sargent)—*Library Journal*, 25:64 [Conference, June 7–12, 1900.]

PICTURES in Library Work for Children, The Place of (Annie C. Moore)—*Library Journal*, 25:159.

READ, Some Things a Boy of Seventeen Should Have Had an Opportunity to (H. L. Elmendorf)—*R. of Rs.* (N. Y.), 28:713.

READER, The Modern Child as a (Tudor Jenks)—*Book-Buyer*, 23:17.

READING for Boys and Girls (E. T. Tomlinson)—*Atlantic*, 86:693.

READING for Children (H. V. Weisse)—*Contemporary*, 79:829.

READING, On (Georg Brandes)—*Internal. Quar.*, 12:273.

READING, On the Pleasure of (Sir John Lubbock)—*Contemporary*, Feb., 1886.

SCHOOL, The Novel and the Common (Charles Dudley Warner)—*Atlantic*, 65:721.

SCHOOLS, School-books, and School-masters. A Contribution to the History of Educational Development in Great Britain (W. Carew Hazlitt)—London, 1888.

SCHOOLDAYS of Eminent Men (John Timbs)—London, 1870.

SHAKESPEARE for Children (Charles Welsh)—*Dial* (Chicago), May 16, 1907, in answer to SHAKESPEARE, Reading, to Children (Walter Taylor Field)—*Dial* (Chicago), May 1, 1907.

STORIES to Children, How to Tell (Sara Cone Bryant)—Houghton, $1.00 net.

STORY-BOOKS, Children's (F. Maccuun)—*Liv. Age*, 241:746.

STORY-TELLERS, About Old (Donald G. Mitchell)—Scribner.

WOMEN'S CLUBS, How, May Help the Library Movement (E. G. Browning)—*Library Journal*, 24:—suppl. C. 18. [Conference, May 9–13, 1899.]